# CATCHING

# OUR DREAMS

## EXPLORING AMERICA BY

## RV

**Sandra Randles**

i

CATCHING OUR DREAMS

Exploring America by RV

CreateSpace

Nonfiction / Travel Memoirs

ISBN-10: 1481054783

ISBN-13-9781481054782

# DEDICATION

To our grandchildren, Christopher, Vincent, Alex, Lindsay, Brandon, Brady, Brooke, Alyssa, Jay, Ella, and Jaxon.

May all your Dreams come true!

# Catching Our Dreams

# INTRODUCTION

This book tells of some dreams that belong to my husband and me, dreams that turned into great adventures.

Our biggest and some say craziest dream was to sell our house and live in a motor home full time. Having the freedom to roam the roads of America and enjoy nature, stand on mountain tops, and to cross great rivers.

For three years we were homeless, at least of a traditional home. We made our home in a RV and enjoyed this great land. It took a great deal of planning and it also took the right timing. We have great memories of our three years on the road. The following pages tell of this time in our lives.

We continue to dream, who knows, maybe someday we will return to the road. You may have dreams too. Go for them, and don't let your memories become bigger than your dreams. "IF YOU CAN DREAM IT, YOU CAN DO IT."

Catching Our Dreams

# ONE

My husband Don is a dreamer. His motto is, "if you can dream it, you can do it." Maybe not today or tomorrow, but with some planning he believes your dreams can come true. This philosophy has come true many times in our lives.

I was brought up in a middle class family in Barberton, Ohio. I would dream of many faraway places, but believed that only the very rich could travel abroad. I was wrong about that because eventually I did travel abroad and I wasn't rich.

My love of travel started when I was very young. During my father's vacations from work, my family traveled around the United States and camped in a tent. I loved camping and seeing all the sights of the places we visited. (We went to Florida and Maine and all the places in between.) My favorite trip was a trip west to Utah. Being out in the fresh air and feeling so at home with nature was where I felt the happiest. Little did I know all the traveling that was ahead for me.

After marrying my husband in 1965 and having four children, traveling was not on our mind or in our budget. We managed a few family vacations and even some camping trips.

First we started out in a tent. Tenting is a lot of work, and with four little ones we often came home more tired than before we left. Then we bought a pop-up trailer. This seemed to be only slightly easier. The children were still very young and most of the setting up and taking down, packing and unpacking, was done by Don and me. Our camping trips were few and far between. Finally we bought a truck camper and enjoyed a vacation to the Florida Keys with our two youngest children, Debbie and Rob.

While I was
alligators, dolphins, an
oceans, everglades, and
intensified.

Our youngest son
after graduating from
stationed in Germany for
there, his first son was bor
didn't take long for the
grandson started to overtak
dream it, you can do it." In
were on our way to German

At the time it wa
would be on such a journey
off of the plane there was
traveled with Rob and his
Forest; we took a boat ride u
toured several castles. Could
away from home? It was n
dreamed of doing.

Returning home and
and home routine after sucl
difficult. Don worked as an

Chrysl
a wee
nurse,
week.
Hawa

We t
Hawa
helicc
climb
We s
renta
highl
birth

hard
The
quic

saw
suff
He
his

3

er Corp. and sometimes worked seven days

k. I worked in a nursing home, as a charge

working twelve hour days, three days a

It wasn't long before our next dream began.

ii, "If you can dream it, you can do it."

In 1996 we fulfilled our Hawaiian dream.

oured four islands, Oahu, Kauai, Maui and

ii. We flew over an active volcano in a

pter and walked through a rain forest. We

ed Diamond Head and visited Pearl Harbor.

norkeled in the clear blue waters and took our

l car on the forbidden road to Hanna. The

ight of our trip was celebrating my 50th

day dinner in a beautiful garden in Paradise.

After each dream was fulfilled, it got

er to return to our routine of work and home.

days were long and hard and our minds were

k to begin our next dream.

As I was working at the nursing home, I

an elderly man lying lifeless in his bed. He had

ered a massive stroke and was unable to move.

could no longer talk or share his dreams with

wife. His wife sat daily at his bedside. As I

4

entered the room the wife asks me about our recent trip to Hawaii. I told her the highlights. She said "Jim and I always wanted to go there, but I guess we waited too long and now it's too late." I've heard this many times in my career. Couples who have put off their dreams, waiting, waiting for what? After my shift ended I went home and told Don of the conversation that I had with Jim's wife. We have so many more dreams to fulfill in our life and I don't want to regret not doing them. We are beginning to talk of an early retirement, but first Europe. "If you can dream it, you can do it."

In May of 1999 we took a two week tour of Europe by bus. We started in London, England. We walked the streets of the city seeing the changing of the guards at Buckingham Palace, visited Hyde Park, the Tower of London, and Westminster Abbey. Three days later we were crossing the English Channel and on our way to Paris, France. I had a hard time believing that I was in Europe let alone on top of the Eiffel Tower. Next we went to Lucerne, Switzerland. This has to be the most beautiful place in the world. It is located in the

Swiss Alps, and it took my breath away. Then we went on to Venice, Italy where we rode a gondola. We also visited Florence, Pisa and then Rome. In Rome we visited the Coliseum, the Vatican, and threw our coins in the fountain of Trivia.

We then left the tour in Rome and extended our stay another week. We rented a car and drove to the city of Pompeii, where we spent the day exploring the ruins. Next we went to the city of Sorrento, where our room overlooked the Mediterranean Sea. From there we toured the Amalfi Coast. The Europe adventure was one, that to this day, I have a hard time believing happened. We dreamt it and we did it.

Shortly after returning from Europe, I read a book about a couple that sold their home, quit their jobs and began their adventure of full time RVing. This seemed like such an exciting lifestyle, to travel all the time. No alarm clocks, no more mowing grass or shoveling snow, doing what we wanted, when we wanted. This was nothing short of an endless vacation. I told Don about the book and some of the adventures this couple in the book had. His reply was "we can do that." "IF YOU CAN DREAM IT, YOU CAN DO IT."

In the summer of 1999 we began shopping for our next home. We decided on a 1999, class A, twenty-nine foot, Holiday Rambler RV. It had everything in it including the kitchen sink. It had a queen size bed in the back, a small but complete bath, and a kitchen with all the appliances including a microwave. It also had a couch and above the dash a small TV. It seemed to have adequate storage space. There was storage in what is called the basement (the compartments under the whole coach). There was also storage under the bed and under the dining table benches. It contained plenty of cabinets and two closets. The thing that excited me most was the huge windshield. I could just imagine looking out as we drove along the highways and byways of America.

I always thought I could be very happy in a tent, with very little in the way of comfort. After seeing all the motor home had to offer and since we were talking of living in it as our only home, I had to admit, I loved it. Don is for traveling in

7

comfort. He liked the modern conveniences that our motor home had to offer. We had a large fresh water tank, propane gas for cooking and heating, a generator to provide electricity anywhere.

This new home had all we needed and much more. We could hardly wait to begin our travels. We named our new home "The Dreamcatcher."

The next step in working toward our dream was to put our home of twenty years on the market. This was somewhat hard since this was the home we raised our children in, but our desire to travel full-time was greater than the sadness of giving up our home. In the fall of 1999 our house had a "for sale" sign in the yard.

After thirty-two years at Chrysler, Don announced he was ready to retire. "Well," I said "if you're going to retire, I'm not working." At the end of October 1999 we both retired at the age of 53.

Our children gave us a retirement-farewell party. Many of our friends and relatives came. I remember my uncle saying to me "What do you

want to retire for? You retire and you'll just die."
"No" I said, "we will retire and live our dreams."

Sometimes our planning and God's planning is not the same. Our dream to sell our house and travel was not to be just yet. My mother was sick and in a nursing home, and the house was not selling.

We planned a trip to Texas to visit Don's parents. They had recently moved to a retirement community and they were excited to show us their new home. Since we no longer had to rush back to jobs, we took two weeks and enjoyed the sights in Texas.

We spent a few days in San Antonio where we visited the Alamo and strolled along the River Walk. The River Walk is a network of walkways along the banks of the San Antonio River. It is lined with shops and restaurants.

We also became acquainted with many of Don's parent's friends, having dinner with them and playing cards.

Upon returning to Ohio, we began the process of getting rid of everything we could live without. There was really very little that we needed. We had a moving sale, and gave much of our furniture to our children. It wasn't as hard as I thought it would be. I am not a keeper. I often get rid of things that I no longer want or get tired of. Don on the other hand had a few things he couldn't part with. He loves automobiles and auto racing. He belongs to SCCA (Sports Car Club of America). During the summer months he works at the racetrack and does what is called flagging. He also owned a race car and drove it a number of times at Mid-Ohio Race Course in Lexington, Ohio. He couldn't part with his car or his collection of numerous tools. We rented a garage and stored a few antiques and keepsakes and of course the race car, car hauling trailer, and tools. We only kept in our house what we needed to live while we figured out our next step.

In December of 1999 we decided to give the Dreamcatcher a trial run. We took it to Florida to spend the Christmas holidays. We also changed realtors hoping to at least get an offer on the house.

Don had no trouble driving the RV. To me it seemed so big and wide and I found it intimidating. The first night we stayed near the entrance to the Blue Ridge Parkway in Virginia. It was very cold and we used our furnace all night. We were not far enough south for camping in December.

We left camp about 9a.m. the following morning and drove to our next stop just south of Savannah, Georgia. We camped our second night at Fort McAllister Historic Park. It seemed like a nice park but it was raining.

We reached Florida on our third day and stayed at Orange Grove RV Resort in Buena Vista. We went to Disney World on Christmas Day. The temperature was very cool and my heart just wasn't in it. Although we had celebrated Christmas with our family before we had left home, gathering together for dinner and exchanging gifts, it was the time of year to be together.

We decided to go further south to find warmer weather. We went down to the Keys for a few days and then back to the Everglades. We were keeping in contact with our children and with my brothers and sisters. My mom's health was declining and I felt the need to be with her. We left Florida and started for home. We arrived home on January 24th.

I was glad we had a home to come to, and glad it was warm and dry. I spent most of the next three weeks at my mother's bedside, with my father and siblings. My mother died on February 10, 2000.

Looking back on that time of my life, I have come to realize a few things about myself. At the time of our Florida trip and trial run with the Dreamcatcher, I was running away. In my career, as a nurse, I had dealt with a lot of death and grieving, but never my own. I didn't want to face what was for sure to come with my mom. I lost my mom slowly as Alzheimer took over her mind. By the time we retired she no longer knew me and had had two strokes. I realize now that, due to guilt, my heart was not in the first RV trip we took. I felt guilty for not staying home and facing what was sure to come.

My mom and dad taught me to love God and my country. They were the reason I had such a desire to travel and spend time with nature. I wanted to get away from this hard time in our lives. What I should have done was to stay home and be at her and dad's side. I also realize now that as humans, we are sometimes weak. I can't change those years but I can enjoy all the wonderful places this country has to offer. The country my parents taught me to love.

"To everything there is a season, a time for every purpose under heaven." Our house sold the first week of March. It was time to start moving the rest of our belongings from the house and to finish loading the motor home. There was so much to do.

We needed to be able to receive our mail while on the road. We contacted a private mail service and arranged for all our mail to be sent to a rented box. They agreed to forward our mail every few weeks to any place we happened to be. They would send it general delivery. We could pick it up at the main post office of any town in America.

13

We went looking for a car to tow behind the motor home. We wanted something we could have fun with that would go anywhere. We settled on a Jeep Wrangler with a canvas top. We thought we would like the fact that we could put the top down and enjoy the sun. (At this time of year we wanted sun). We also bought a tow dolly, a two wheeled trailer, to haul the car behind the motor home. We attached a bike rack to the back of the Jeep, and loaded our two bikes. All together from front to back it measured about forty five feet.

We bought our first computer. It was a lap top. There was no room for anything any larger. In the year 2000 there was no such thing as Wi-Fi. You had to be someplace that had a telephone and use dial up. I wasn't sure how often we would be able to get online, and besides we knew very little about computers. Mostly we wanted it to email our children. We also bought our first cell phone. When we went to get it they gave us a map of areas in the U.S. that had no signals. Technology has improved greatly since then.

Our next step was planning our route. We didn't want to follow any schedule since we had all the time in the world. We did have one destination in mind and that was Alaska. March is too cold to head in that direction so we decided to head to Texas again to visit Don's parents.

We bought a Trailer Life campground guide and became members of the Good Sam's Club. Good Sam's gives you discount rates at several campgrounds and also sends you an RV Magazine every month with lots of useful information.

We said our goodbyes and promised to be back in Barberton sometime in the late summer, but just to visit. Saying goodbye to the grandkids was the hardest. There were seven of them at the time. Also it was very hard saying goodbye to my dad. But he gave us his blessing and told us to go and have a good time and enjoy our retirement.

We were very excited to be on the road and on our way to CATCHING OUR DREAMS!!!

# TWO

Finally we were on the road. It was March 16th and the rain was coming down on our big windshield. It was hard to imagine that this was our new norm, driving down the highway on our way to nowhere. We really didn't know where we would be that evening nor did we care. We made no reservations because we weren't sure how far we would travel that first day. There was no place we had to be and no timeline to get there.

The nice thing about traveling in a RV was the fact that our whole house was at our fingertips. If Don wanted a soda from the fridge, I just got up from my large comfortable seat and on shaky legs went to the back and got it. It's not easy walking in a moving motor home. I think it's called getting your "sea legs." I held on as I walked for fear of falling. Also if I was cold and needed a sweater, I just went to the closet in the back and got it. I even tried going to the bathroom while we were moving, but I wouldn't advise it.

When it was lunch time we pulled into a roadside park and made a sandwich. The sun was out and the spring flowers were starting to bloom. After stretching our legs it was time to get back on the road.

We stopped for the night at a place called Beech Bend Park. It is located in Bowling Green, Ky. It is a private RV park with what is called full hook-ups (electric, sewer, and water). We made dinner on the grill and took a walk around the park. We stopped and talked to other campers and listened to their tales of travel, and of course told them of our new lifestyle.

The next morning we were anxious to get on the road and on with our adventure. After a good breakfast, we were on the road again. We were then in the central time zone and the temperature was much warmer. We spent our second night in Grenada, Mississippi. We looked at our map in the morning and noticed that we would be going through the town of Vicksburg. We stopped to visit the National Military Park and Cemetery. They charge an entrance fee at most National Parks but if you buy an annual pass it is good at all National Parks for one year. We were not sure where our travels would take us, but thought this would be a wise investment. After enjoying the park and having lunch we continued on our way. It was 6 pm by the time we reached our next camp in Louisiana. From there we went to La Grange, Texas for a quick overnight. As we drove south in Texas, the trees were getting smaller and smaller. Cactus was blooming on the side of the road. On March 20th we arrived at Split Rail RV Park in Mission, Texas. We planned to spend two weeks with Don's parents in the Rio Grande Valley.

Mission is a small town near the Rio Grande River at the southern tip of Texas. Even in March, the temperature was near 100 degrees. There were very few homes with grass in their yards. Their yards consisted of gravel and cacti and tropical plants. The town is 80% Hispanic. It is a great retirement community. Some come to stay there and live, while others come as snowbirds or as they call themselves "Winter Texans." The area is noted for its year round growing season and its citrus trees.

Don's parent's house was a small ranch style house within a retirement community. They had a gravel yard and two citrus trees in their backyard, one orange and one grapefruit. The grapefruit were huge and very sweet. At the side of the house there was a huge poinsettia plant that was as tall as I am, with flowers larger than dinner plates. I've always heard that they grow everything big in Texas, now I believe it.

My husband and I are explorers and we wanted to explore the Mission area. We tried many Mexican restaurants and we especially liked one located on the Rio Grande River. It is called Pepe's. They have the best nachos and margaritas. Also on most afternoons they have a band and dancing.

One afternoon we went with Don's parents to Pepe's for lunch and to take a boat trip down the Rio Grande River. As they started the paddle wheel of the boat, rubber tubes flew out the back of the boat. The captain explained that in the early morning hours many Mexicans came across the river to work in the fields. They would strip off their clothes and put them in a plastic bag to keep them dry. Then they would swim across the river in an inner tube; hide the inner tubes, dress, and go to work. At the end of the work day they would retrieve their inner tubes, swim back across the river, and return home. What a hard way to live.

As we cruised up the river the captain pointed out many sights, birds, plants, and trees. The landscape was very flat and you could see far into Mexico. We passed a park on the Mexican side of the river; the captain explained that during many celebrations they hang piñatas, from the mesquite trees, filled with candy for the children.

Suddenly the captain yelled out "Ladies, get your cameras and focus on the left side of the boat." We all grabbed our cameras and turned to the left. In the water were three young Mexican men. They were swimming in inner tubes with their plastic bags filled with their clothes held high above their heads. As we approached they stood up and lowered their inner tubes below their waist. One never knows what you will see when you are exploring.

While we were staying in Mission we also explored some areas throughout the Rio Grande Valley. On a day trip we visited Santa Ana National Wildlife Reserve. We rode a wagon through the park and enjoyed a guided tour. On the same day we continued east to South Padre Island. The Beach was beautiful with sand as white as snow and water a clear blue-green color. We had dinner at a restaurant overlooking the Gulf of Mexico. It was a great day and we returned to our RV and slept very comfortably in our air conditioned home.

No trip to southern Texas is complete without crossing the border to Mexico. However, we were advised not to take our car over the border. We parked our car on the U.S. side of the river and walked across the bridge to the town of Progresso. As we neared the Mexican side, there were several children, some very young, maybe three or four years old, with a cup in their hand begging for a "big nickel" (a quarter). As we entered the town we could see many shops and street vendors selling their goods to tourist. There was a Mexican boy, about six years old, dressed in rags, with a cup in front of him. He was singing the Italian song "O Sole Mio," how could you not give him a "big nickel?" We bought a few souvenirs after bartering with the shop owners and then had an authentic Mexican meal and of course a margarita. It was a fun day and we again went home tired.

The two weeks went by very fast. We enjoyed the time we had with Don's parents, meeting their friends and seeing the sights, but we were ready to find out what else Texas had to offer. We spent the last day in Mission doing laundry and saying goodbye. We also picked a bag full of the wonderful grapefruit from the tree in the backyard to take with us.

On April 4th we were heading west. Our next destination was Big Bend National Park. We traveled 325 miles that day and arrived at Holiday

Travel Park in Del Rio at 5:30 pm. We fixed a relaxing dinner and went to bed early. The next day we arrived at Big Bend N.P.

Big Bend N.P. has some of the most outstanding scenery in Texas. It is located on the bend of the Rio Grande River, and contains acres of river, desert, and mountains. The mountains are the Chisos Mountains; the whole range is within the park boundaries. The desert is part of the Chihuahuan Desert. It is wild and yet beautiful.

We decided to stay in the park even though they had no hookups. This is called dry camping. We used our generator for electric and pumped water from our fresh water holding tank.

We had a large gray water holding tank (for bath and dish water), and a large black water holding tank (sewer). We could camp about 3 or 4 days before we needed to empty these tanks or longer if we were very conservative.

We arrived in the late afternoon. The camp was very crowded. It was sunny and about 70 degrees. The campground is located in a part of the park called Rio Grande Village. The scenery was

24

beautiful and the cacti were in bloom. We set up camp (put our awning out) and fixed dinner on the grill. When we were done eating, we noticed several large animals roaming the campground. They looked like big pigs with a rat like nose and no tail. I often heard that everything is beautiful in its own way, but these creatures were just plain ugly. They started toward us so we climbed on top of the picnic table. I wanted to get my camera but was afraid to get down. As we looked around the campground we noticed that no one else seemed to be paying any attention to these creatures. We got down from the picnic table and got the camera from inside the motor home and took a few pictures of these "pigs."

We learned from the other campers these ugly pigs are called Javelinas. They are scavengers and hang around for table scraps and garbage. We were also told that they aren't pigs but members of the peccary family. They originated in South America. As far as I was concerned they could turn around and go back. There was at least a herd of 12 or more roaming around this camp and they made me very nervous.

After the Javelinas went about their business, we drove the Jeep to a nearby lookout and watched a beautiful sunset. After returning to camp we did some reading and went to bed. I have to admit I had some nightmares about our after dinner visitors.

In the morning we decided to move outside the National Park to a private RV park. We searched in our Trailer Life Camping Guide and found one with full hookups and it even had hookups for cable TV. Now this doesn't matter to me, but, like I said, Don likes all the modern conveniences, and we both like keeping up with the news.

After getting settled in our new camp, we went back to Big Bend to explore. First we went to the visitors' center and got some maps of roads and trails. We also bought a National Park Passport. It is a blue book that you carry with you to all National Parks and get it stamped to keep a record of all parks you visit. We planned to fill this book.

We walked many desert trails. Our favorite was called the Santa Elena Canyon Trail. This trail has canyon walls that loom over a thousand feet above the Rio Grande River. We crossed a creek and climbed several stairs and descended into a canyon along the Rio Grande. How can anyone see such beauty and not believe that this world was created by an awesome God?

As we were driving on dirt roads through the park, we saw jackrabbits, roadrunners, coyotes and large lizards. Don spent many hours on our hikes looking for snakes, scorpions, and tarantulas but couldn't find any, of which I was glad. After three days at Big Bend we were ready to move on. I still had not gotten used to the fact that we were not on a vacation and we had no reason to hurry.

We wanted to head north in the direction of Alaska.

Next stop, Alaska!

The Rio Grande River at Big Bend, N.P.

Javelinas in Our Camp Ground

28

# THREE

As we headed north, we stopped to explore the city of Santa Fe, New Mexico. We had visited this city while on vacation several years before; we loved the city and wanted to visit again.

Santa Fe is located in the foothills of the Rockies. No lack of sun in this city, it shines 300 days a year. The streets are narrow and winding with very old adobe buildings. The historic buildings have been converted into shops and restaurants.

We went into town to go through the shops and to have dinner. We bought an Indian dream catcher to hang in our motor home.(Quit appropriate, I think.) We also bought a Kachina Indian doll. I thought I would like to collect these dolls. Looking back I wonder what in the world I was thinking. We lived in a 29x8ft space, why would I consider collecting anything?

After a month on the road, I still found it hard to believe that this was now our home.

After leaving Santa Fe, we stayed at Homasa Meadows RV Park north of Durango, Colorado. We arrived in the early afternoon. It is a small park, but has full hookups and a coin operated laundry facility, that by now we needed. The park is located on the Animas River and was very quiet and peaceful. The next day we took the Jeep into the city of Durango to explore.

Durango is located in southern Colorado, in the Animas River Valley, surrounded by the San Juan Mountains. It is where many movies were made. "Butch Cassidy and the Sundance Kid", "City Slicker", "National Lampoon's Vacation", and "How the West was Won" are just a few. And it is also the original home of the Rocky Mountain Chocolate Factory; of course, we couldn't resist buying some chocolate. (It is an old western town with many shops and restaurants, and we had fun exploring it.)

We went to the Durango and Silverton Narrow Gauge Railroad Museum. The railroad was constructed to haul silver and gold ore from the San Juan Mountains, but it didn't take long for people to realize that it was the view that was the real treasure. The railroad is called narrow gauge because the tracks are 36 inches apart compared to the standard gauge of 56 inches. They offered a train ride into the mountains, but it was too late in the day so we bought our tickets for the following day.

In the morning we arrived at the train station early, dressed in layers. It was sunny and 70 degrees, but we were going up into the mountains and we were advised to be prepared. Since we were going to be gone most of the day, we packed a lunch. We were ready for our ride back in time.

In the summer months the train travels from Durango to the historic mining town of Silverton. Since this was only April, it only went as far as Cascade Canyon.

We traveled around the mountains and across wooden bridges high above the Animus

River. The view was breathtaking and as we traveled along the mountain edge we wondered what kept the train from falling into the canyon below.

We stopped for lunch along the river far into the wilderness of the San Juan Forest. It was beautiful. We sat on a rock beside the river and ate our lunch as we listened to the water running down stream. Mountains were all around us and blue sky above. While we were eating our lunch, the steam engine was being refilled with water. After lunch, we climbed back on board and returned to Durango.

It was a great day and we vowed to someday return during the summer months and take the train all the way to Silverton.

Our next destination was Mesa Verde National Park; it is within 50 miles of Durango. We arrived in the morning and, after getting settled in our campsite within the park, we went to the visitors' center to find out information about the park and to get our N.P. passport stamped. Mesa

Verde is high in the mountains and the air was cold. In Spanish, Mesa Verde means "green table."

The park is located in the four corners area and was established in the early 1900s. Within the park there are hundreds of cliff dwellings and archaeological sites.

We decided to take a ranger guided tour to a cliff dwelling called Cliff Palace. The one hour tour began at a lookout. The trail gradually wound down the side of the cliff to the dwelling. It was amazing to see this ancient dwelling on the side of the cliff. How did these people live in such a place, how did they build it? As the ranger answered our questions I began to have problems of my own.

I began to cough and started having a hard time breathing. The combination of the high altitude, sage in bloom and the cold air was a bit too much. I just wanted to get out of there, but the rest of the tour involved climbing five 8-10 foot ladders.

While wheezing and coughing, I managed to reach the top and returned to the car. I know that this sounds crazy, the temperature was in the 40s, but I needed the air conditioning to help my breathing. Sometimes things don't work out the way we plan; this was one of those times.

After a short rest we took some self guided tours of these wonderfully preserved ruins. This area of our country is so well preserved and we are grateful to have visited them.

We returned to camp and, since we were dry camping, we started the generator. We ran the furnace until we went to bed. We covered ourselves with a lot of blankets and wore our hooded sweatshirts to bed. The next morning we awoke to a layer of SNOW on the Dreamcatcher.

As I said before, our plans and God's plan are not always the same. It was too early in the year to be in the Rocky Mountains and we headed southwest to the desert. We took a break from our trip north to let the season catch up to our dream, a break to relax and play.

We stopped at Four Corners. It is the only place in the U.S. where 4 states (Arizona, New Mexico, Utah and Colorado) come together in one place. We stood in four states at one time. Four

Corners is in a very remote region and is managed by the Navajo Nation. They sell their crafts on the side of the road. We stopped to browse; after all, I thought I might find a pair of turquoise earrings. They wouldn't take up much room.

From Four Corners, we traveled to Page Arizona. We stayed at the Lake Powell Campground at the edge of town. It had full hookups, cable TV, swimming pool and a laundry facility. It was hard to believe that just that morning our RV was covered in snow. By the time we reached camp, in the middle of the afternoon, the temperature was 75 degrees and sunny.

What a difference a few hundred miles in the right direction makes. This life style allows the changing of our environment within hours. What's not to love?

Page is located in the Lake Powell region. The Glen Canyon Dam forms the reservoir on the Colorado River known as Lake Powell. The lake is on the borders of Arizona and Utah. This area is absolutely gorgeous. Most of the lake is surrounded by red canyon walls.

We took a boat tour of the lake and made a stop in an area you can only get to by boat. We got off the boat and took a trail that lead to a place called Rainbow Bridge, a red rock natural arch.

The water of Lake Powell is clear and blue with red canyon walls. We stayed in Page for three days relaxing and trying to take in the awesome view.

We hiked some trails that went along the edge of the cliff above the river. On one of the trails we saw a Diamond Back snake. Don tried to get a picture of it, but he couldn't get close enough. That's one picture we could do without.

I could talk about Lake Powell all day and still could not express its beauty. I guess the only way to understand, what I am trying to say, is for you to go there yourself.

We next drove through Zion National Park in Utah; the views in the park were spectacular. The ranger had to block off traffic that was coming from the opposite direction so we could drive down the middle. Our rig was too wide to share the road with oncoming traffic through a tunnel. This tunnel had windows in it and you could see out the side of the mountain. The roads in the park twisted up and down the mountains and the view was great.

From Utah, we traveled to Las Vegas, Nevada. We stayed in North Las Vegas. The park was called The Hitching Post. It was a great park except it had noisy jets flying overhead day and night. We stayed four nights. We visited the casinos, had a picnic in Valley of Fire State Park and to Don's immense delight, we went to Las Vegas Speedway and saw the IRL Indy Car Race. Our time was filled with warm and sunny days and we both enjoyed our visit.

One thing that is quite different, when traveling full time in a RV, is that we were unfamiliar with the best places to go for certain services such as haircuts.

We were used to getting our hair cut by our daughter Debbie. She is a beautician and knows how we like our hair, but she was back in Ohio.

We drove into a plaza with a salon and Don went in for a cut. He came out looking like a punk rocker. His hair was spiked straight up and sprayed so stiff it wouldn't lay down even after covering it with a hat. I laughed so hard. I guess the next time it would be wise to ask a local (with a nice haircut) to recommend a barber. My advice is "if you ever go to Las Vegas, get your hair cut before you go."

Don wanted to go see London Bridge. "London Bridge?" I said. "What are you talking about?" He went on to tell me that someone had bought the bridge from the city of London, England, and brought it to the United States. "Is London Bridge not in London? Why didn't I know this? I went to school in Barberton, Ohio. Why didn't they teach me this?" The London Bridge of our childhood song, (London Bridge is Falling Down) is not in London, but is right here in our own country.

We left Vegas and traveled to Lake Havasu to see the bridge. Lake Havasu City is located on the Colorado River on the border of California and Arizona. The lake is a large reservoir behind the Parker Dam.

We set up camp at Havasu Falls RV Park. This was a very nice park with full hookups and a pool. It also had a room where we could plug in our computer to get online. We spent some time emailing home and then went to town to explore.

London Bridge was built in London in the early 1800 and spanned the River Thames. It was dismantled in 1967. (So that's why I didn't learn about it in school, it was moved after I graduated.)

The Arizona bridge was purchased from the city of London by Robert McCulloch. He had the external blocks from the bridge numbered, dismantled and transported to America to construct the present bridge in Lake Havasu City.

When you are traveling around this great country, you learn something new every day. Around every corner is something so amazing and wonderful. I awoke every morning and wondered what the day would bring. I was always pleasantly surprised.

Santa Fe, New Mexico

Cliff Palace in Mesa Verde, N.P.

# Catching Our Dreams

Durango Train Ride

Red Rock Arch at Lake Powell

Catching Our Dreams

London Bridge in Havasu City

# FOUR

After leaving Lake Havasu, we headed north to a park just south of Flagstaff to explore the town of Sedona. It is located in the Arizona High Desert, under the towering southwest rim of the Colorado Plateau. It is characterized by red rock formation and is at the mouth of Oak Creek Canyon. The beauty of these canyons in the western states are, without doubt, some of the most breathtaking scenery in our country. I never got tired of exploring them. The town of Sedona is filled with shops and art galleries, and we spent hours browsing through them.

We returned to the Dreamcatcher for a peaceful evening of relaxing around a campfire and visiting with our campground neighbors.

After a wholesome breakfast, the following morning, we went on a loop road in our Jeep. The loop road took us to two National Monuments. The cost to take the road was $5, but with our National Parks pass we were waved by without paying.

The first monument we came to was Sunset Crater. This area has large cinder cones formed by extinct volcanoes, even though it erupted hundreds of years ago, it still remains without vegetation. The color is black with patches of reddish brown lava and ash.

The other National Monument on the loop road was Wupatki National Monument. This is an amazing area with many preserved ruins of ancient Puebloan People. There are several ruins scattered over a large area of the desert northwest of Flagstaff. We felt blessed to have visited these amazing sites.

While we were in this area, we couldn't pass up the opportunity to visit Grand Canyon National Park. We had visited the park twice before but seemed drawn to see it again. The grandness of the canyon is a view that is awesome the first time you view it and just as grand the next time, and the next as well. We drove home (home is where you park it) through the forest. We saw antelope, mule deer, and elk. Mule deer have large mule-like ears and are about 3 1/2 feet tall. They look almost comical with their big ears.

We continued onward through Monument Valley to Moab, Utah. Monument Valley is located on the border of Arizona and southern Utah, and lies within the Navajo Nation. The red rocks with its towers and formations are very outstanding, and it is the setting for many western movies. The Navajo word for Monument Valley when translated means "valley of the rocks."

We stayed at Riverside Oasis RV Park just north of Moab, arriving about 5 pm. It was sunny and warm and 80 degrees. We put our awning out and fixed a simple dinner. We had traveled over 300 miles and decided to walk around the campground and stretch our legs. You can find out a lot about a town by talking with other campers. We learned that the campground was packed because they were having a custom car show on the following Saturday. This seemed to make Don feel very lucky since we just happened to be here for this event, lucky us.

While I was still working, some people asked me how I would be able to live with my husband in such tight quarters, day in and day out. Well, so far it has been so wonderful sharing all the sights and the adventures of being on the road. It is a give and take situation. I really don't enjoy looking at old cars, but I can give up one afternoon. When I need my space, I just take a walk or jump on my bike for a ride around the camp. Don enjoys evenings watching TV and I grab a book and get lost in it. So far, this has not been a problem. I'll let you know how this works out down the road.

The first full day in Moab we went to Arches National Park. We drove through the gate and showed our pass. We had packed a lunch and drinks and were off to a good start. Arches N.P. is known for preserving over 2000 natural sandstone arches. There are some Ute petroglyphs on some of the rocks and we stopped to walk a trail to see them. When we returned to the Jeep we continued on our auto tour of the park, suddenly the gas warning light started beeping. We were just about out of gas. "Oh no, how could this be?" This place was so beautiful and all we could think about was running out of gas. There is nowhere to buy anything in the park. The tour was only about 25 miles into the park and 25 miles out. Since we were about half way through the park we decided to finish the road tour. The scenery was breathtaking and we finished the tour, but we both agreed it would have been a better day if we hadn't been worried about the Jeep running out of gas. This is definitely a park to tour again at another time. When we left the park we still had a ways to go to get back to town. We made it to town with few fumes in the tank. Lesson: check your gas gauge before entering a National Park.

On Saturday, after stopping at the post office to pick up our mail, we went to the Rod and Custom Car Show in the city park. Then it was time to do something that I enjoyed, so we went downtown to browse the shops. I bought an Indian doll called Gentle Brook; since our youngest granddaughter, at the time, was named Brooke I had to have it. There I go again; collecting things we don't have room for. We then enjoyed a dinner at a sidewalk cafe. To Don's delight, the cars from the Custom Auto Show paraded the streets while we ate.

The following day we went to Canyonland National Park (with a full tank of gas). This park is also located near Moab. The area is formed into canyons, mesas, and buttes by erosion caused by the Colorado and the Green Rivers. On top of the mesa, "Island in the Sky," we could see both rivers in the canyon far below. We hiked a few short trails and I wanted to take the Jeep down the side of the cliff on a four wheel drive trail. Now you have to understand that Don is afraid of heights and he was too nervous to drive down the trail, so I drove. It was very steep and very nerve wracking, but we made it into the canyon. We had a picnic lunch by the river and saw Mule deer and one mountain goat.

I didn't know what would still be ahead for us on this adventure of ours, but thus far, Moab was my favorite. This part of our country is so unlike the eastern states. When the red rocks glowed from the sun shining on them, I felt like I was on another planet.

Our next stop, on May 2nd, was a park 200 miles to the north in Vernal, Utah. The park we stayed in was called Dinosaurland K.O.A. It was a nice park with all the necessities plus a pool, laundry facilities, cable hookup for the TV, and a modem in the front office for the computer.

Every morning brings a new adventure. The adventure for this day was to explore Dinosaur National Monument. It is located on the border of Colorado and Utah in the Uinta Mountains. We stopped at the visitors' center to get a map of the park and also to get my N.P. passport stamped. We took some hiking trails and found some fossils of dinosaurs embedded in the red rock cliffs, and also saw some petroglyphs. We stopped for a picnic lunch and then drove the back roads to our home on wheels. We had to drive slow and stopped a few times because it was open range in that part of the country and cattle were often in the road.

The next day I cleaned house on the inside and Don cleaned the outside. This didn't take long, as you can imagine.

Then we were off again, this time to Flaming Gorge Recreation Area. We took along a picnic lunch and enjoyed eating while overlooking a beautiful lake in a red rock canyon at the Dam of Green River. On our outing we saw 42 elk, 11 mule deer, and one mountain goat. It is awesome to see these animals roaming free in their natural habitat.

We were soon on the road again and headed to Salt Lake City. The trip from Vernal to Salt Lake is about 175 miles through the mountains. Don thought it was a good idea for me to spend some time each day driving the motor home. "What if I break my leg and can't drive for several weeks?" he said. Well, I never thought of that, "O.K. I'll give it a try."

After stopping for lunch in a church parking lot (it's a good place to stop if it's not Sunday), I got behind the wheel. Wow, this thing was big. I felt like I was taking up the whole road. I managed to drive for about an hour and then I was ready to give it up. I don't know who was more nervous, Don or me. It was difficult to look at the scenery and drive at the same time. I preferred relaxing in the passenger seat and looking for animals. That night we stayed in a nice RV park in Salt Lake City.

We went for an informative and interesting guided tour of the Mormon Temple. (Temple of the Church of Jesus Christ of Latter Day Saints). The Temple is located in the center of Temple Square and is seen above all the buildings in Salt Lake City. It is 223 feet high and contains 253,015 sq. feet. It is of Gothic architecture and took over 40 years to complete.

The gardens in Temple Square were gorgeous. The Mormon Temple is the home of the Mormon Tabernacle Choir. The art work of the 11 foot marble statue of Christ was amazing. This tour was remarkable, informative and very educational.

The weather the following day was 70 degrees and raining. The one thing we enjoyed doing on a rainy day was traveling around in our Jeep and seeing area sights.

After doing our laundry, we were off to see the Great Salt Lake. I was there as a child and can remember swimming in the extremely salty lake.

We then took a ride north to the Golden Spike Historic Site. It is the site where officials of the Central Pacific and the Union Pacific Railroad met in 1869 to drive four symbolic spikes [two gold] celebrating the completion of the first transcontinental railroad.

After another good night's sleep, we again hooked up the Jeep and headed further north into Idaho. We stayed at Boysen State Park. As we were driving into the park we saw a 3 foot long snake on the road leading into the campground. Now I know that there are snakes everywhere in this great country, but I didn't like one greeting us as our welcoming committee. Again, I am glad that we were not in a tent.

The campground is on the banks of a reservoir. It was cloudy and raining and about 60 degrees. The ranger came around and collected the nightly camping fee and drove off. As it got dark, we noticed there were no other campers in the park, no lights anywhere and it was very dark. Don fell asleep fast (how do men do that?), but I stayed awake for hours hearing all kinds of unfamiliar noises. When morning came, I was ready to move on.

After looking at our map, we saw that Yellowstone National Park and Grand Teton National Park were across the border in Wyoming. We headed in that direction.

First we wanted to stop at a park in Thermopolis, Wyoming. We only traveled 27 miles to get there, but at least it was a lot nicer park and there were lots of other campers and no visible snakes. The park was in the country and surrounded by farm animals. It was located on a river and was very peaceful and quiet.

Having arrived early in the morning we took the time to wash the RV. This home on wheels has a huge windshield and therefore attracts every bug that God had created; at least that is the way it looked. The temperature was only in the

40's but the sun was shining and there was very little wind, the perfect day for a ride. We ask the employees in the front office for information on things to see in the area and they were very helpful.

We packed a lunch, made sure there was plenty of gas and we were off to explore once more. First stop was Hot Springs State Park. We hiked some trails and saw the world's largest hot springs. We ate our lunch at a picnic area then moved down the road to the Wyoming Dinosaur Museum, where you can go on a dinosaur dig for $100 for a day. We didn't go, but the museum was informative and a good way to spend a chilly afternoon.

Our next stop was Ponderosa Campground in Cody, Wyoming. It is a good RV park with all the hookups. The cost was $116 for the week and that included cable TV. This was to be our home base for the following week. There was a lot to see in that part of the state and we wanted to see it all.

We began our week of exploring by visiting the Buffalo Bill Museum in Cody. This took a few hours, and reminded me of the old westerns my brother used to watch when we were young. Now the difference between the time I can go through a museum and the time it takes Don (who stops to read every little thing) is quite different. By the time we finished, we were ready for lunch. We went into town (it looked like something out of those old westerns), and entered a saloon (like out of those old westerns), and had a sandwich and a beer. The weather was cold and windy and 45 degrees. We had no place we had to be and had the afternoon to waste (gotta love this lifestyle), so we drove 50 miles to the entrance of Yellowstone Park.

Just driving to the entrance was an adventure in itself. We traveled along the Shoshone River through a beautiful canyon. Along the way we saw buffalo roaming in the fields just like in the days when Native Americans hunted them for food and clothing. Wow, they are big animals; their heads were just enormous.

We stopped the Jeep and Don got out hoping to get a picture. There was a buffalo, right along the road,next to the guard rail. There are signs along the road warning not to get too close to these animals, they may charge at you. Don kept trying to get closer and closer and I was getting very nervous. Finally he took the picture and returned to the Jeep, I left out a sigh of relief. We also saw some moose and deer. I cannot get used to seeing animals of the west and northwest roaming free and living as they should without fences and without boundaries. Right then, I could see that was exactly how Don and I were living in this dream of ours, no boundaries. This was a great day and we felt blessed.

The next day was Saturday and the duties of housekeeping and laundry had to be done. The laundry didn't take long since there were four washers in the campground laundry house, and neither did the housekeeping.

We went into town and saw people lining the streets. We asked others what was going on. We were told that once a year a stampede of wild horses are brought into town to be auctioned off, this was the day. As we stood on the edge of the road we could hear the roar of horses' hoofs coming toward us. We saw these beautiful animals being led by cowboys on horseback. This was a spectacular sight. Wild horses have a beauty all their own.

We then went out to dinner at a western style steakhouse called "Cassies". We ended the day by going to an old fashioned movie theater and saw "The Gladiator."

The next three days were spent exploring Yellowstone Park. Yellowstone was the first National Park in the world. It is known for its wildlife and geothermal features, especially Old Faithful Geyser.

Taking the paved drive through the park we saw free range bison, wolves, elk, deer, black bear, and grizzly bear. We took some hikes on wooded pathway built over the geysers, saw waterfalls, and snow capped mountains. Of course, we stopped and waited for Old Faithful to erupt.

Every once in awhile when we were driving, we would come to a place where the traffic would be stopped, most of the time it was when an animal like a grizzly bear was near the road. This is called a "Bear Jam". It was wonderful to see these huge animals in the wild.

We then came to an area where the forest was obviously burned. A large forest fire had gone through the park in 1988 burning about a third of the forest and the loss of so many trees was still very visible. It was very depressing to see such a large area burned to the ground. Fortunately the forest floor was turning green again. We were told that the first sign of life to return after a forest fire is the beautiful magenta flower of a plant called "Fireweed." Nature is so amazing.

On one of our daily tours we went to a park adjacent to Yellowstone, called The Great Tetons, National Park. We drove through the park and enjoyed the snow capped mountains and lakes. We live in such a beautiful country and we were anxious to see more.

It was fifty miles, from our home base in Cody, to the Yellowstone entrance. We both agreed that we enjoyed the journey getting to the park as much as we enjoyed the park. Many animals we saw were on these back roads. On our last visit to the park we saw two large grizzlies right outside the entrance. They were walking right along the road. AWESOME!

We left Cody, Wyoming and visited Little Bighorn National Monument. (Custer's Last Stand). We went to the visitors' center and saw a movie on the history of the battle that took place on this land in 1876.

The area memorializes the battle between the U.S. Army's 7th cavalry and the Lakota and Cheyenne warriors. The battle was fought along the ridges and steep bluffs and ravines of the Little Big Horn River. It was one of the Indians last armed efforts to preserve their way of life.

As we stood on top of Last Stand Hill, with the tall grasses blowing in the wind, I could almost hear the cries of the wounded. There were white markers where the solders fell. It was a very moving experience.

We continued to drive through the rolling hills and farmlands of Montana. As we were traveling on Rt.12 out of Helena, there was a large herd of cattle being driven by cowboys on horseback, down the middle of the state highway. Now that is a scene not seen in the East.

Also very unique to the Rocky Mountains is a wonderful fruit called huckleberries. We made some stops for huckleberry ice cream, milkshakes, pies and anything else huckleberry. Umm, umm good.

We arrived in Glacier National Park on May 23rd; it is located in Montana, bordering Alberta and British Columbia, Canada. It's a large park and includes two mountain ranges and several lakes. Glacier National Park borders Waterton National Park in Canada and the two parks are known as the Waterton-Glacier International Peace Park.

It was about 70 degrees and sunny. We parked the motor home, climbed into the Jeep and went exploring. The mountains had snow on top and the lakes were crystal clear and cold. We hiked a few trails, and expected to see some animals, maybe some elk or bear. We didn't, but we still had a very exciting time.

There was a manhunt in the park with a lot of police and road blocks. They were looking for a man named "Joe." Apparently he had kidnapped a woman, let her go, then ran into the woods in the park. Well, from that point on we stopped looking for bears, etc. and started searching for "Joe." We were stopped at a roadblock and they searched our car. Now if you know anything about a Jeep Wrangler you would know that you can't hide anything in it. They ask us a few questions then we were on our way.

We enjoyed the many waterfalls, lakes, and mountains with glaciers.

Every day is a new adventure and I could hardly wait to see what was on the road ahead. When we left the area, the next day, they still had not found Joe, the fugitive.

Stampede of Wild Horses in Cody, Wyoming

American Buffalo in Yellowstone, N.P.

Geysers at Yellowstone, N.P

Sandy at Canyonland, N.P.

Don on Arch in Canyonland N.P.

Sandy Driving Jeep into Canyon

# FIVE

When our children gave us our retirement party, we received many useful gifts, much needed gas cards, books on travel, bird books, and insulated travel mugs. The one thing that was very special to me was two houseplants from our son, Tim. He had planted two plants in one container. The container was made of plastic and had suction cups on the side. He said we could stick them to our window and not worry about them tipping. What a great gift for someone on the road, and they made the Dreamcatcher seem even more like a home. Twelve years later I still have those same houseplants in our home.

As we came closer to the Canadian border, I started to worry that the border guards might take my beloved house plants. I took them off the window and put them in the storage space under the bed. I didn't know what the rules for transporting plants across the border were, but I wasn't taking any changes.

On May 25th, 2000 we crossed the Canadian border. Crossing the border pre 9/11 terrorist attack was relatively simple. We stopped at the border and the border guards asked us a few questions and waved us on. My plants were safe.

Our first day in Canada the temperature was 13 degrees centigrade and we had to get accustomed to buying gas by the liter. Canadian money at the time was about 48%. I decided I needed to carry a calculator the next several days.

We arrived at our camp in the early afternoon. It was called Mountain Shadow Resort located just south of Radium Springs, British Columbia. We were surrounded by large beautiful snowcapped mountains and tall pines. This camp was not an easy camp to get the motor home into. The campsites were level and tiered up the side of the hill, like steps. After disconnecting the Jeep at the office, we were able to maneuver the Dreamcatcher into place. Following a walk around the camp (a good exercise on the side of a hill), we made a campfire to cook dinner. After we ate, we sat around the campfire for a while. The air was cool and it was very peaceful. I wanted to roast marshmallows, but of course we were out of them. We walked to the camp store at the foot of the hill. No marshmallows. They had sold their last bag. We walked back to camp disappointed. About a half hour later the campground owner appeared with some marshmallows for us. He had gone into town to buy some for us. We had to admit the owners of this campground were great hosts.

The following day, we slept in and ate a breakfast of bacon and eggs. We left camp with the Jeep in tow and headed north up route 93. This route is also known as the Icefield Parkway. It is in the Province of Alberta and goes through Banff National Park and Jasper National Park. It can snow on this road anytime of the year. We were lucky; it was a beautiful, sunny, cool day. This was some of the most spectacular views I have ever seen. Snowcapped large mountains, many with glaciers, and the water of the streams and lakes were a beautiful aqua color, and cloudy in appearance (no pollution up there). We saw many animals as we traveled. Spotted deer, bighorn sheep, elk, mountain goats and two black bears; their coats were deep black and shiny.

Our next stop was south of Jasper. We parked our RV in the midst of tall northern pines. The camp had full hookups. "Great." There were elk in the campground. We were told that they come to the tall pines, in this camp in the spring, to have their young. They could be very aggressive if anyone would get too close to them. There was an elk near our site, curled up under a tree. What a magnificent creature. As I watched her from our dining area window, I was in awe of nature and all of God's creation.

The rain started to fall as we went to bed. There is nothing as peaceful and relaxing than rain hitting the roof of the Dreamcatcher in a quiet forest.

Memorial Day weekend was here and we had to find a RV park with a cable TV hookup. The Indy 500 auto race was on and, of course, it is a must see event. After some research, we found a park just west of Prince George, British Columbia. I could care less, but this made my auto racing loving husband very content. It was a very cloudy weekend and only about 48 degrees. It was a good day to relax and read a book and maybe take a nap.

I'm not much of a nap person but I hadn't been getting much sleep. I've always been an early riser, usually with the sun. In this part of the world, at this time of year, the sun rises at 4am and doesn't set until 10:30pm. We had two skylights in the RV, one in the shower and another in the bedroom. I put some black paper over the skylight hoping to darken the bedroom as much as possible. Hoping it would give us a better night sleep.

A must have for traveling the Alaska Highway is a publication known as "The Milepost." It was first published in 1949 as a guide for traveling the Alaska Highway (referred to locally as the Alcan). It has since expanded to cover all major highways in the northwest corner of North America and is updated annually.

We made it to mile "0" of the Alaska Highway, Dawson Creek, B.C. The official end to the Alaska Highway is at mile marker 1422 (96 miles from Fairbanks). We parked our Dreamcatcher at a RV park called "Northern Lights." So many people were heading to Alaska in RV's, we were lucky to get a campsite. We called ahead to the next three spots to make sure we'd have a place to stay.

We went into town to have our picture taken at mile marker "0". Then we went to the visitors' center and saw a movie on the making of the Highway. The Highway was built during World War II for the purpose of connecting the contiguous U.S. to Alaska thru Canada. It was completed in 1942 and at the time was 1700 miles long. Due to rerouting and straightening it is now 1387 miles long. It became a public highway in 1948. The historic mileposts are used to denote major stopping points along the way including mail delivery.

While we were at Dawson Creek, we had lunch at a restaurant called "Alaska" and went grocery shopping. We weren't sure of the wilderness ahead of us, but we thought it was a good idea to stock up on supplies. We found an organic bakery and bought some delicious German rolls that tasted similar to the ones we had in Germany in 1992. Umm Good!

On June 1st we traveled to mile marker 277 and stayed at a place called Huskies 5th Wheel RV Park near Fort Nelson, B.C. The weather was sunny and warm and many of the same RVer's that were in Dawson Creek were also at this park. We had a good day on the highway and the road so far was paved. We were driving through the forest, most of the day and were certainly "away from it all." We only passed a few crossroads that had what they called a lodge and the rest of the drive was through the forest.

We stopped for lunch at a roadside pull off and ate food from our fridge. We came upon a so called lodge and went in for some ice cream. It was a very rustic place.

In the early afternoon we saw a large moose cross the road in front of us. I love the fact that we never know what we will see next and what the next day will bring. We don't waste our time thinking of the "what if's" in our journey, but just enjoy every second of every day.

Our second day on the Alaskan Highway didn't go so smoothly. There was a lot of construction and unpaved road. The RV and Jeep were covered with dust. We got a second chip in the huge windshield of the Dreamcatcher and after traveling the dusty roads we were in need of an air filter, and there was no place to buy one. Wilderness, Wilderness, Wilderness. We did see a black bear, caribou, and deer while traveling. That alone made the day worth every mile.

At one point we stopped along the road to check on the Jeep. Don had left the door open and in flew a bird. I screamed and the bird was scared, flopping all over the dashboard. We opened the windows and door and Don even tried to catch him in his cowboy hat. Just as I remembered to grab the camera, he flew out the window. Don reported that the Jeep had two broken fog lights, but I didn't care. I was just glad that the bird was free.

We made it to the next camp at mile marker 632.5. We unhooked the Jeep and backed into our site. I got out of the RV to help direct Don as he backed up. I was on the passenger side and didn't see what was on the driver's side. Bang!! He hit a tree; the Dreamcatcher had its first scrape. We both agreed that it gave it a little character.

Most people who are traveling toward Alaska in motor homes arrive at camp, set up their RV, hook up to water and electric, then pull out their lawn chairs and watch the other travelers arrive. Of course everyone was watching us as we hit the tree. We have had better days, but all of it was worth it just to be in such an incredible place and living our dream.

We were becoming familiar with a few of the couples and spent our evenings talking with them about their day and ours.

This camp had a RV wash and car wash. We spent the next morning washing the vehicles. I wasn't sure if this would do much good because we had many miles yet to go on this highway, but it makes us feel better to be able to start off clean on the next stretch of road.

During the making of the Alaska Highway in 1942, a U.S. army GI posted a sign with his name and hometown, others would pass by and add their signs.

Today the tradition continues. It has become a place travelers on the Alaska Highway put up a sign to tell others they have passed that way. It is known as "Sign Post Forest." There are now thousands of signs in this forest. People from all over the world have posted their signs. Some are made out of wood, cookie sheets, pans or whatever they could paint their name on.

We wanted to make ours out of wood but we had a hard time finding the materials we wanted. We went into the Town of Watson Lake and after much searching we found a hardware store and some wood and paint. You would think that after all the years people have been doing this that someone would be nearby selling what you need to make a sign.

We went back to camp and Don made our sign. Our sign said "Randles, Catching Our Dreams 2000, Ohio." Then we went to the forest and nailed it to a post. If we head to Alaska again we will make our sign before we leave home, where we can buy our material from a super large home improvement store.

Our third day on the highway was nice with only a small amount of construction. Gas seemed very expensive at $1.93 a gal. We stopped for lunch along the road. As we were eating two other RV travelers, that were at the last couple of camps, passed us and honked their horns and waved.

Traveling the Alaska Highway in a RV is like traveling in a caravan. The same people moving along at about the same pace. The towns and camps are about a day's ride apart. If there is much to see we all stay a couple of days to explore.

We stopped for the night just south of Whitehorse, Yukon Territory at mile marker 911. The campground is a large gravel parking lot, but it does have full hookups and cable TV.

Whitehorse inhabits about 2/3 of the population of the Yukon Territory, and is the territorial capital. They have a camping supply store and we went into town to buy an air filter for the Dreamcatcher.

If we travel this road again we will be sure to bring extra air filters for the vehicles. Everything seems to cost so much more up there, if you can even find what you are looking for.

We spent the evening in town seeing a vaudeville-style "Frantic Follies." There were girls, with colorful skirts, dancing in chorus lines to music and poems of Robert Service. The stories and dress was from the Yukon Gold Rush days.

The next day we went to the grocery store. This is one town that has a large store. Since we left the "lower 48" the stores have been small with very limited variety. At home the cereal aisle has more than 50 different kinds of cereal; up here they maybe have six, if you're lucky. Fresh fruit and vegetables were very hard to find; they didn't look too fresh and were expensive. Also, milk only lasted about four days after you bought it. I wonder how the people up here eat enough to get fat to keep them warm in the winter. I began to miss fresh fruit. At home in June the strawberries were ripe. I missed them that year.

In the afternoon we went for a ride to nearby Mile Canyon. It's a recreation area a few minutes from town. The scenery was spectacular with a suspension bridge over the Yukon River. From the bridge you get an awesome view of the canyon below. Then we took a leisurely walk on a trail along the river. We returned to camp at 11pm. It was still light outside and I found it hard to sleep, but Don had no problem.

Some travelers at this point decide to leave the Alaskan Highway and travel the "Top of the World Highway." It goes to Dawson City and on to Alaska Highway 9. We decided to continue on the Alaska Highway to Tok, Alaska. I really wanted to see what was ahead on both highways, but we had to choose one. Maybe on our future travels we will try the other.

The next day we felt more alone. The remoteness and the extremes of the northern climate, results in many surprises along the way. We drove along the beautiful Kluane Mountain

Range and Kluane N.P. The snow covered mountains were amazing. Our camp for the night was on Kluane Lake and was a government campground; it is the largest lake in the Yukon Territory and is located near Destruction Bay.

About two miles from camp two very large grizzly bears were on the road. Don stopped along the side of the road, I grabbed my camera and took a picture from the dining window of these two huge, wonderful creatures. We were the only ones on the road and it was complete wilderness. I expected Grizzly Adams to come out of the forest at any time.

As we arrived at the park we noticed no one else was around, not even a park ranger. We picked out a site near the water. A reservation at this camp was not needed, it was clear. We were alone, us and the grizzly bears. We walked around the camp and gathered up some firewood. There were over 100 campsites and not one other camper in sight.

We built a campfire on the water's edge and cooked hamburgers and hobo pies. I was looking over my shoulder frequently expecting the grizzlies to come as uninvited guests. The sun set at 1:30am. We had to cover our blinds on the bedroom windows with black garbage bags to block out the light. The night darkness would only last a few hours. It would be getting light at 3am. It was way too quiet to sleep, at least for me.

This wilderness makes me realize how very large the world is and how small we are. There was nothing around us for miles and we were all alone.

The next day on June 7th we arrived on the border of Alaska.

Jasper, N.P. Alberta, Canada

Mile "0" of the Alaska Highway

Sign Post Forest near Watson Lake

Grizzlies near our camp at Destruction Bay

11.30pm with the sun still high in the sky. Don lights the campfire at Destruction Bay

# SIX

At the "Welcome to Alaska" sign we stopped to have our picture taken. We made it. It was a long way from the start of our journey and our dream, but we were standing in Alaska and again on U.S. soil. There had been a lot of construction on the highway and we still had to drive over 100 miles to the first town, and the place where we spent our first night in the "Land of the Midnight Sun" (Now I can really identify with this phrase).

About 125 miles inside the border, we came to a town called Tok. Tok originated as an Alaska Road Commission Camp for the construction of the Alaska and Glenn Highways in the 1940's. Tok is the only town in Alaska that the highway travelers must pass through twice, once when arriving and once when leaving.

Our campground for the next two nights was named Sourdough Campground and is located just south of town. We set up camp in the tall northern pines and got ready to go out to dinner to celebrate our arrival. I called home to talk to our children and then placed a phone call to my, then 89 year old, dad. "Hi dad" I said. "We made it to Alaska." "You're in Alaska? Are you on that cell phone?" he asks. "Yes," I replied. "It sounds like you're right next door," he said. He started laughing. I said "What's so funny?" "Well, you don't even have wires on it; doesn't anything get in the way between there and here?" Oh he would be so amazed in today's world of technology.

We went to town and ate at a restaurant called Fast Eddie's and then returned to our camp to get some rest. The next day we would start to explore this great land. It was quiet and peaceful in this camp and I no longer felt that we were the only two people on earth. We finally made the bedroom dark enough and I think this time I was the first one to fall asleep.

The town of Tok is the trade center for the Athabasca Native villages. Many of the local native arts and crafts can be found in the gift shops. We toured these shops and walked around town. Don wanted to go panning for gold so we bought a pan and listened to the shopkeeper's tips for gold panning. Getting in the Jeep we headed up the Taylor Highway for a day trip to the town of Chicken.

Chicken was once a mining community in the gold rush days of the late 1800's and is rich in history. Chicken got its name because early miners could not agree on the spelling of ptarmigan, a local chicken-like bird. It is a national historic site and home of two gold dredges from the mining era. We felt sure that the gold miners missed some of the gold and left some for us.

Chicken is a small town in the middle of the wilderness (of course). It has a population of 37. As we entered  town, we saw a small (and I do mean small) post office. Across the street were three buildings hooked together with a common wooden porch. The buildings were very rugged and historic looking. Town consisted of a mercantile emporium, a saloon and a cafe.

As we walked into the emporium, the lady behind the counter (at least I think she was a lady), asked where we were from. As I looked up, I noticed this woman had a beard. Now I don't mean a little hair on her upper lip. I mean a good week or more growth of beard. It was hard not to stare at her. (She definitely needed some hormone therapy). OK, I thought, the natives up here are a little different than the people from Ohio. I continued to have a conversation with her as if I didn't notice a thing. She was telling how much work it is to get ready for the tourist season and then she told me this story.

"A few nights ago, when I got home from work, so tired I could hardly move, I got into my hot tub. I was just starting to relax, when out of the woods came this big old grizzly bear. Of course I had my rifle right there beside me," she said. "Sure," I replied, trying not to look too shocked. "Well," she continued. "I had to shoot him, and I didn't want to, because you know how much work dressing out a bear is."

Down in the lower 48 you don't even dress out a chicken let alone a bear. I go to the meat counter and buy a boneless, skinless chicken breast. Dress out a bear, are you kidding me? Well, I answered her with "of course." She also told me that the lady that runs the cafe has a 10 year old son that has a bear print on his bedroom window and he won't let his mother wash it off. This Alaska life is not for sissies.

We finished looking around town, (by that I mean the other two stores), then returned on the same road that we had used to enter Chicken. Usually we try to take a different road home to see something different, but up in Alaska there are very few roads.

On our way back down Taylor Highway, we crossed a small creek. Don pulled the car off the road and we got out to pan for gold. Don seems to really have gold fever. Does he think it will just appear along the highway? He did find two small pieces about the size of a grain of sand. We returned to Tok, and the shop owner said it would take about a beer can full to be worth $27,000. He then advised us to buy a book that will tell us where we can pan for gold. Being the good tourist that we are and wanting the best chance to find gold, we bought one.

The next day, on June 9th, we took Route 2 to North Pole, Alaska. The day was the warmest day that we have had since we were in the deserts of the Southwest. It was a sunny day and 80 degrees.

The park we stayed in was called Santaland RV Park. It was looking a lot like Christmas around this place. They had reindeer behind fences, (reindeer are elk that have been domesticated) and a toy store with, who else but, Santa himself. The streets of North Pole are decorated with holly, candy canes and lights. It is where the spirit of Christmas lives year round.

Talking with other campers, we learned there was a salmon bake not far away in a park called Alaskaland in Fairbanks, where we decided to eat dinner. They cooked the fish over charcoal and it was fantastic. Fairbanks is Alaska's second largest city and they don't even have a Walmart. Other than that, it was just like any other large city.

The next day we returned to Fairbanks and took a three hour river cruise on the riverboat called Discovery. The tour was given by Alaskan Native guides. It included a tour of a Chena Indian Village, including huts with sod on the roofs. (How do they mow the grass on the roof and how do they get the mower up there?) We also visited the kennels of four-time Iditarod winner Susan Butcher. I enjoy these informative tourist places to learn about the history and the area, but I look forward to seeing more of this land on our own.

We wanted to see what lies ahead on the road north of Fairbanks. We left North Pole and went about 10 miles northeast of Fairbanks to the small community called Fox. The campground is called Northern Exposure and is the last RV Park north of Fairbanks.

We wanted to drive to the Arctic Circle (160 miles from Fairbanks) on the Dalton Highway. We had heard many things about this highway. The Dalton Highway follows the route of the Trans-Alaska pipeline. It goes from Fairbanks to Prudhoe Bay on the Arctic Ocean (about 500 miles). It is mostly sharp rocks, gravel, and mud. There are no gift shops or service stations, just tundra and mountains. It has large pot holes and many trucks travel this road at 50 miles per hour on their way to Prudhoe Bay. Knowing all this, we still wanted to go to the Arctic Circle.

We filled our gas tank before we started out (good idea) and packed some food. We weren't worried about getting back before dark since it didn't get dark. It seems odd to us that it was so warm out and we are wearing shorts and tee shirts. We can see the pipeline to our right as we head north. It is suspended off the tundra to protect the permafrost and for animal migration. It appears much larger than I thought it would be. We were glad we had the Jeep on this rough gravel road.

About half way to the Arctic Circle we came to a pull off. The area had picnic tables, so we got out of the Jeep and had our lunch.

The Tundra is beautiful in its own way. The ground is permafrost, which means the subsoil is permanently frozen. How can this be when the temperature is 80 degrees?

We had our binoculars and took some time looking over the vastness of this region. I walked around and noticed some wildflowers and moss growing on and around some rocks. There was only one other car in the parking lot, then they drove away. I felt alone and yet comforted by the beauty and stillness of this region.

We could see a herd of caribou in the distance. Walking on the permafrost is like walking on a big sponge. You sink in with each step. We returned to the Jeep and continued on our way.

When we reached the Circle we found a turnout in the road, a large sign that says Arctic Circle and a rustic looking outhouse. We got out of the Jeep and took a picture by the sign.

Most of the world has not laid eyes on what lies beyond this attraction, in the land known as the "Last Frontier." I have never experienced such solitude and tranquility. We saw only tundra in all directions and were completely alone.

After several minutes of taking it all in, we returned on the gravel road to civilization.

Our next adventure would be Denali National Park. By the time we awoke the next morning, the sun had been up for hours. (I wonder if it ever goes to bed.) At about 10:30 in the morning we drove the RV down Route 3, the only road to Denali. It was cloudy, cool with sprinkles of rain when we arrived. I don't know what happened to the 80 degree temperature we had the day before, but as we headed south, it was much cooler.

The word Denali means the high one. The Alaskan Range contains North America's tallest peak, Mount McKinley at 20,329 feet. The park is surrounded by mountains that go on forever and water that is fresh and clean. It is six million acres of wild land, wild flowers and most of the park is tundra.

We wanted to camp in the park, but was told that we would have to wait two days before there would be a spot available. We put our name on the waiting list and went down the road to a private RV park called Denali Grizzly Bear Campground.

After setting up camp, we went back to the park to explore. We went to the visitors' center and signed up to take a bus tour into the park the following morning. There are 91 miles of road in the park, but only a small portion of it is paved, due to permafrost, and you can only take your vehicles the first 15 miles. We entered the gift shop where they were selling bells to attach to your hiking stick to scare bears away. Well this seemed like a good idea. I think we should get one. Maybe we will pick one up in the morning. We drove the 15 miles into the park and saw a mama red fox under a bridge with her two pups, so cute.

We returned the following morning to take the bus tour. A park ranger gave a talk on some things we could expect on our day's journey. He also advised us not to buy the bell in the gift shop for our hiking sticks, "bears are curious animals and will come looking for the sound" he said. Well, that is good to know. Makes you wonder why they would even sell them.

   I'm not real fond of bus trips, but it was the only way to see the park, so off we went. It was a 4 hour drive to an overlook called Eielson, where we were given a box lunch and then we returned on the same road. While we were at the overlook, we could see hundreds of caribou in the valley below. Also on our tour we saw grizzly bear, elk, moose, dall sheep, and golden eagles. I think it would have been more fun to explore this area on our own, but rules are rules.

   Due to the rain and clouds we were unable to see Mount McKinley, maybe tomorrow.

   The next day we moved into the park and stayed at the Teklanika River Campground. We set up camp and took a walk around the camping area to talk with others. We relaxed and took in the beauty of this place; the snowcapped mountains were breathtaking. After lunch, we decided to take a hike up the creek that was near our campsite. It seemed like a good idea at the time.

As we walked near the water we headed toward a bridge that was a ways down from the campground. We looked back over our shoulder from where we had just been, there taking a drink from the creek was a huge, and I do mean huge, blonde grizzly bear. He was too close for comfort for me. We decided to head across a field to the road; at least there we could flag down a car for help. As we tried to run toward the road we found it difficult to get anywhere fast due to the permafrost ground. With every step we took, we sank in. It was like walking on a sponge.

I remembered reading on the park pamphlet, that "a grizzly can run 35 miles an hour, and the wildlife is worthy of respect." My question was would the wildlife respect me?

We looked back over our shoulder several times to see if the bear was following us. He was still drinking, and walking slowly in our direction. I just couldn't walk fast enough and it seemed like I was in slow motion.

Don's mom's advice to me when we left Texas was if we were chased by a bear I just needed to stay ahead of Don. Well I wasn't doing a very good job of that. We finally reached the road and when we looked back the bear was still at the creek. We at last felt safe. We returned to camp by way of the road.

At one point I truly believed that I was going to be eaten by a bear in Denali National Park, and was very grateful that we did not buy bells for our hiking sticks. We tried again to see Mount McKinley before we left the park, but again it was hidden by clouds.

We were then headed to Alaska's largest city, Anchorage. What awaits us there we're not sure, but this wilderness land seems to have surprises around every bend. We stopped at a town called Willow to camp for the night and do laundry.

After our chores were done, we went for a ride to find a creek for panning. We found one along a side road. I took out my folding chair and a book and Don went to work to find our fortune.

A car pulled up beside us and asked "Do you mind if I ask what you are looking for?" Don replied "I am panning for gold." "Oh," she said. "Do you mind if we take your picture?" "No, go ahead." Don replied. He proceeded to bend over with his back to the lady and filled his pan with water and sand. "Snap" she took the picture of Don's backside with his pants sliding down showing his "Maytag Repairman Smile." (If you know what I mean). They will go home from their vacation and show their pictures to all their friends and there will be Don's backside.

Like I said, you never know what is around the next bend. The only wildlife we saw that day was a porcupine. We didn't find our fortune, but we put a few more grains of gold in our vial.

We moved on down the road to a RV park just north of Anchorage. It was sunny and about 65 degrees. This large city constitutes 40% of Alaska's population. The very unique visitors' center is in the middle of the city. It is a log cabin with tall northern pines surrounding it. It has a grass roof and has beautiful flowers everywhere. If you would take a picture of it and showed it to someone they would think that you were out in the back woods and not in the middle of Alaska's largest city.

This city has many parks with trails and sometimes a bear or elk wanders into town. It is urban and yet wilderness.

We went to a park near Cook Inlet called Earthquake Park. The park commemorates the historic 9.2 magnitude earthquake that happened on Good Friday in 1964. Tsunamis caused most of the damage elsewhere in the state, but landslides caused nine deaths in Anchorage. This park is a memorial to this historic quake.

While in the city we walked around and visited many of the shops and had dinner.

On the outskirts of town is a Walmart store, we hadn't seen a Walmart since we left the lower 48. I felt like I was a kid in a candy store, so many selections to choose from. We bought supplies to restock our home and many extras, not knowing when we would find another store with so much to choose from. At home you take for granted these superstores, but up there in the northern wilderness, they are few and far between.

Traveling south from Anchorage on the Seward Highway we came to a fork in the road, one leading to Homer and Kenai on the Sterling Highway and one leading to Seward. We choose first to go to Homer.

Homer is the southernmost town on the contiguous Alaska Highway system, and is literally at the end of the road. We camped just north of town, and spent the evening walking around the camp and talking with other travelers. The scenery was awesome with snowcapped mountains across the bay and bald eagles flying overhead.

The next day was the summer solstice, and I didn't think we would see even an hour of darkness. I tried to stay up all night to find out. I fell asleep at 3AM and woke at 5AM only to find the sun still shining. The night was without darkness.

We then went to explore what is known as the Homer Spit. (A spit is a finger of land extending out into the water.) The Homer Spit is a narrow 4.5 mile long gravel bar that extends into the water. On the spit is the Homer Harbor with very rustic looking little shops, art galleries and restaurants.

There are many charter boats for fishing for halibut, salmon and whatever else they may be able to catch. We stood and watched as they brought in the day's catch. They would hang these large fish up to be weighed. One man had a 176 pound halibut. He was having it cut up and packed on ice and sent to his home in the lower 48.

We then had lunch on the spit, and of course we had fish and chips, as they say up there "Just for the Halibut." Yummy!! It was a nice place to spend the day, with glaciers in view and eagles soaring overhead.

They have many celebrations on the day of the summer solstice and one was a midnight mountain climb. We skipped this fun sport and returned to camp. At midnight the sun was shining bright and children were playing on the playground. This is a strange and wonderful land. I dozed lightly that night and every time I looked out the window the sun was shining like it was the middle of the day.

Returning to the Sterling Highway, the next day, we traveled north on the Kenai Peninsula, stopping to watch the fisherman catching salmon from the Kenai River. There were so many fisherman standing in the river, it is a wonder they could catch anything.

A lady standing on the shore caught a large salmon as we looked on in amazement. She yelled over her shoulder to her husband, "Hey, now I have to go get a fishing license." Well, now where I come from we get our license before we pick up our poles. Is it different here in Alaska?

We traveled down a side road toward the fishing village of Kenai. We were spending the night at Captain Cook's Recreation Area located at the end of that road. It is a park in the woods with no hookups; it is located on a cliff above Cook Inlet. It is a nice park with shade and fishing and it seemed like a great place to relax.

We set up camp and went for a walk down a path to the beach. As we were walking through the woods, we saw many wild flowers (forget-me-nots, blue bells, prickly rose, star flowers,

101

miniature dogwood and chocolate lily). I am so amazed at the beauty of these flowers, in the woods, in this wilderness. As we walked the trail I realized that I am getting to be an expert at identifying animal droppings, elk, bear, etc. Don comments that I know my sh__. I guess that is a compliment.

In the evening we walked to the edge of the cliff, located behind the last row of RV's, to see how far we could see from our perch. I would say that I am a person who can find God's beauty in so many things, a child's smile, a flickering candle, or even a dandelion, but I have never seen anything like what we saw that night.

Sometimes God's beauty is something very outstanding. I will try to describe it as best I can. As we approached the cliff's edge we could see the mountains on the other side of the inlet with their snow covered peaks. Looking to our left, we could see the Kenai River. Far beyond that was the Homer Spit, that we had left hours before. Beyond that was the tranquil blue sea. To our right, was the inlet with tall trees and wilderness. Wow, this was enough for me to be grateful for, when God threw in one more bonus. Two majestic bald eagles, soaring at eye level, straight out from where we were standing. It was a scene that will stay forever in our minds. It brought tears to our eyes and a kind of peace to our souls.

As we were standing there in awe, a lady from our camp approached and exclaimed "I am so bored, it was my husband's idea to come to Alaska and I just want to go home." We could hardly respond to this comment. How could anyone be bored with this view in front of them? I don't know if this woman knows God, but of this I am sure, she is missing something in her life that is keeping her from enjoying this wonder. That I find is very sad.

The next day we were on the road again, this time we went back to the fork in the road and headed to the town of Steward. The days that we have been traveling south, have been cool and about 60 degrees, cloudy most of the time with an occasional sprinkle of rain.

Seward is a quaint fishing town nestled on the waters of Resurrection Bay. It is a picturesque town, flanked by rugged mountains on one side and the salmon-filled Resurrection Bay on the other. It is the only town on the eastern side of the Kenai Peninsula. Seward harbor is busy with cruise ships and fishing charters.

After setting up camp at a park called Bear Creek, we went off to explore the town of Seward. Watching fishing boats come in amazed us. The fish that come out of the ocean are huge. What would it feel like to pull one of those on board?

We decided to splurge that evening and ate at a very expensive restaurant called Ray's. It is located on the water overlooking the bay and we watched sea otters play as we ate a delicious meal.

The following morning, after eating a good breakfast, we returned to town. We bought tickets to go on an all-day boat trip through Kenai Fjords National Park. The "Major Marine Kenai Fjords Tour," which included a buffet lunch with prime ribs and salmon.

This seemed like a great idea at the time, but by day's end I wish we would have stayed on dry land. When we started out the water was calm and the scenery was great. We saw a very colorful bird called a Puffin, a humpback whale, seals, and sea otters.

I didn't know much about glaciers when our tour began. As we cruised slowly along the shore we witnessed glaciers up close and personal. We stood on the deck of the boat and witnessed a glacier calve icebergs into the sea. Large chunks of pale blue ice, making a roar as they fell, one of Nature's best shows.

We also learned about the ice worm. There is actually a worm that spends its entire life in glacial ice, and it comes to the surface in the morning and evening. (I wonder how they know when it is morning when it doesn't get dark).

After eating a buffet lunch inside a warm and comfortable cabin, we went out on the deck once more as we headed for open waters. This is about the time my stomach started to do flip flops. It was windy and the water was very choppy. I spent the rest of the cruise with my head hanging over the back of the boat. The waiter offered me ginger ale or crackers. I just wanted to die in peace.

Couldn't he see I was busy? Don likes to tell people that I recycled the salmon (just doing my part to help the environment). We returned to shore, but my stomach did not return to normal until the next day.

After a good night's sleep and feeling better and back to normal, Don wanted to go see another glacier. I was all for it as long as we didn't have to get there by boat. We drove north of town to a place called Exit Glacier. We had to hike a .8km trail to the glacier. We could feel the cold from the ice as we neared the glacier. The color was a brilliant blue, what a beautiful sight. Again we stood in awe of nature.

We returned to town, had lunch and browsed in several gift shops. I bought an Eskimo doll to add to my collection of things we don't have room for. We ended the day by driving down the coast until the road ended. It was cold, rainy and foggy when we returned to camp. It was great night for sleeping in our darkened room, with the sound of rain hitting the roof.

We next moved to a campground north of Steward on the road to a village called Whittier, located in the Williwaw National Forest. It's a beautiful campground surrounded by mountains, glaciers, woods and streams. I can't seem to get enough of the glaciers. In fact there was a glacier behind where we parked the Dreamcatcher. Awesome sight. Standing right next to it we could actually see the ice worms. They looked like tiny pieces of thread in the ice.

After examining the glacier, we drove the Jeep down the road to a place called Portage Lake. The lake had icebergs floating on top and was surrounded by glaciers. The icebergs were such a beautiful blue and as we stood there looking at them we were chilled. I'm not sure if it was from the cold of the ice or if it was the wonderment of it all.

After stopping at the visitors' center and watching a movie about glaciers we returned to the Jeep and drove to the town of Whittier.

Whittier is on the northeast shore of the Kenai Peninsula and on the west side of Prince

Edward Sound. There is only one road into town and that is through a two mile long combined rail and highway tunnel. When a train is not going through, cars can go through one lane at a time.

The tunnel links Seward Highway with the isolated community of Whittier. This is a small town of about 170 people with about 90% of them living in one huge building that was built post WWII and had been converted to condominiums. We found the town to be a small fishing village and a port for cruise ships to dock so passengers can catch a train to Anchorage and Denali. Fog rolled in while we were there. We couldn't see much of the mountains or the sea so we did what my parents would have done at a time like this. They would have enjoyed an ice cream, and that is exactly what we did while we waited on a train to go through the tunnel before we could enter and return to camp.

We continued north of Anchorage to the Glenn Highway and planned to spend the weekend in the region of Palmer. It was Friday afternoon when we arrived and we drove into the small town of Wasilla. Wasilla is the Iditarod Trail Sled Dog Race Headquarters. We saw a movie at the visitors' center and then we took a ride on a wheeled sled pulled by these outstanding Alaskan huskies. I couldn't resist picking up a husky pup that was wandering around the area. So cute!

We returned to Anchorage to attend the Saturday Market and to have dinner at a place called "The Moose's Tooth" In the evening we went to a place called Ships Creek to watch the salmon fisherman. We watched as the salmon swam upstream, they had even built a ladder to aide them in their journey. This was amazing to see.

On Sunday evening we did something Don enjoyed, an auto race in Wasilla at the North Star Speedway. It's hard to believe that even up in Alaska they have auto racing. It seems to me if there is a race track around Don can sniff it out.

Most things we read about Alaska before this trip, warned of the huge mosquitoes they have. Well, we had not been bothered with them so far and were beginning to think that all those tales were false, until reaching a campground near a town called Glennallen. We drove into camp and parked the Dreamcatcher alongside a creek, nestled in tall northern pines. A beautiful place, we couldn't wait to get out and do our daily walk around the park.

One thing was very strange about the other campers. There were very few people outside, and the ones that were had covers over their faces. Every part of their bodies was covered. "It can't be that bad, we will just spray with a little repellent and go for our walk" I said. Well it was terrible; we were out about 10 minutes and had to run to keep from being eaten alive. We both itched from head to toe. We only stayed one night at this camp. The next morning we left this mosquito infested place without a bit of regret.

We drove up to the town of Glennallen, away from the creek and the campground, and were glad that the mosquitoes did not follow us. There was a Fourth of July parade going on and the road in town was blocked. We parked the RV in a church parking lot and enjoyed watching the parade. The parade was much different from the ones with bands, floats and fire trucks we enjoyed in Ohio. This parade had 4x4's decorated with moose and caribou heads, floats with tents and rugged looking men, and even Smokey the Bear. The only float that looked like the ones from home was a float decorated in red, white, and blue with a lot of children waving flags.

Our next destination was the city of Valdez. It is a two hour drive from the town of Glennallen, on the Richardson Highway. Just when I thought the scenery could not get any more spectacular, it did. As we drove south on this highway there were mountains on all sides. We saw a few animals, a moose and her calf, some dall sheep on the side of the road, and caribou. We went through an area of ponds and marshes and spotted some swans.

As we continued on, we could see the Trans Alaskan Pipeline. This was a very scenic drive. When we came to an area that was wide enough for the RV and the Jeep we stopped and took a break to enjoy the scenery. We could see a blue and yellow train on the other side of the canyon with

111

the words "Alaskan Railroad." It was running on a track on a thin ledge on the side of the mountain.

Next we came to the 7 Mile Hill. This was a bit of a challenge with the RV. I was so glad it wasn't one of those days Don wanted me to learn to drive the motor home. (He seemed to have forgotten about the one hour a day thing and I wasn't going to remind him). At the top of Thompson Pass we could see the view of the valley below.

Next in our view came Keystone Canyon which was very narrow with walls that were straight up and down. Taking the RV through anything narrow is very nerve racking. There were rocks on all sides which parallel the Lowe River with two fabulous waterfalls, Bridal Veil Falls and Horsetail Falls. We made it to the town of Valdez. To this day, I'm not sure how Don was able to maneuver the RV, with the Jeep, down such a steep and twisting road. All I could think of was, when we were safely at the end of the highway, there was only one road out of this town and it was the same one we just came down. We would have to drive this treacherous road again.

Valdez is located on the north shore of Port Valdez in Prince William Sound. There are mountains on all sides and its beauty is breathtaking. In 1898 Valdez was the debarkation point for those traveling to the Klondike Gold Field. The original city was destroyed by a tsunami caused by the 1964 earthquake. It was then rebuilt at a more sheltered location.

We went on a bus tour of the oil terminal, which is the southern terminus of the Trans-Alaska Pipeline. It was also the point of departure for the tanker involved in the 1989 Exxon Valdez oil spill. Three to five tankers depart from Valdez each week and there was one being filled while we were there. The oil travels 800 miles through the pipeline from Prudhoe Bay to the Valdez terminal to be loaded on these huge tankers. A large metal thing, shaped like a bullet and called a pig, is sent through the pipeline to clean it out.

There is a monument to the men and women who built the pipeline with a quote that says "We didn't know it couldn't be done." Construction of the pipeline was started in 1969 and completed in 1977. Amazing what can be accomplished with first a dream and then a plan.

We enjoyed exploring the town of Valdez and watching the fisherman bring in their catch of the day. We browsed in some shops and ate dinner in town.

The following day was warm and sunny, about 75 degrees. We drove to the old Valdez site that was destroyed in the 1964 tsunami. It was located at the edge of the water and some of the evidence of the town remains. It is an eerie feeling to stand on the shores where so many lost their lives.

Since it was such a nice day we took our lunch and drove the Jeep down Mineral Creek Road for a day of exploring. We were driving along and enjoying the beautiful canyon when all of a sudden we were stopped by a snow plow. It was July 6th and 75 degrees, but it seemed an avalanche had blocked the road and it was just then being cleared from this out of the way, dirt road.

Alaska, I love it, you never know what is around the next bend.

After waiting for the road to be cleared, we continued on our ride. We saw many waterfalls and realized this road was a treasure. We were alone on this road. People who just stay on the main tourist routes miss so much. We came upon a peaceful creek with crystal clear water and we again tried our luck with gold panning.

We ate our lunch as we sat by the creek and then I had to go to the bathroom. You men have it so easy when you are in need, but for women it creates a problem. Well I figured everything would be ok. We hadn't seen a living soul since we passed the guy with the snow plow. Wouldn't you know it, as I am getting down to business; a vehicle loaded with people came flying past. I sure can move fast when the need arises.

No gold was found on this adventure but we had a great day and ended it by returning to town and walking a trail at Dock Point Park.

There was one more town we wanted to visit before leaving Alaska and that was Skagway.

To leave Valdez we again had to travel the steep road we came on. As I said before, in Alaska there are few roads and most towns have one road in and the same road out. So we began our climb up this steep, twisting, breathtaking road. The Dreamcatcher was slow moving but managed the climb and we reached the top without incidence.

We continued up the Richardson Highway through Glennallen and stopped again in Tok. We spent the night and did our household duties. Cleaned house, washed the RV and the jeep, did the laundry and grocery shopped. We had to try one more time to pan for gold so we took the road to Chicken and again tried the same creek, but we did not find the mother lode.

To get to Skagway, you actually have to leave Alaska on the Alaska Highway and take it to where it meets the Klondike Highway in Canada, and then take the Klondike Highway south, back into Alaska, to the coastal community of Skagway.

The trip from Tok to our next camp was rough. There was lots of construction between the Alaska border and Destruction Bay. Gravel roads, dust, dust and more dust. All our cleaning of the vehicles was undone, lots of potholes and delays. Dust seemed to enter the Dreamcatcher through every crack and I even thought I could hear her choking at times.

We were back in the Pacific Time Zone for this one day, but we kept our clocks on Alaska Time. We made our camp in Haines Junction, Yukon Territory and recovered by spending our evening in the comfort of our home. Outside there were mosquitoes galore. These were not Alaskan mosquitoes, but Canadian mosquitoes that seemed just as hungry.

Traveling toward Skagway, on the Alaska panhandle we were again in awe of the spectacular scenery. Skagway is a coastal community surrounded by wilderness and located at the northernmost point of the inside passage. It is a popular stop for cruise ships. More than 100 years ago prospectors came through Skagway on their way to the Klondike Gold Fields of Canada.

After arriving in town, and setting up camp, our first priority was to find a place to buy headlights for the Jeep. Both had been broken out by the rough roads. While we were in town we had dinner at a place called Bonanza Bar and Grill. After eating we browsed a few shops and had again bought a few souvenirs.

The town resembles the way it must have looked long ago in the gold rush days. It was very rustic with saloons and stores selling things like Alaskan furs. The town is surrounded by snowcapped mountains and four large cruise ships were in port. This is surely a town for tourist. The shop clerks were dressed in gold rush attire.

The following day was cool, 55 degrees, cloudy with a light rain. We took a water taxi 15 miles up the coast to the town of Haines (359 miles if we would have driven to Haines by road). This time I did not get sick and enjoyed seeing the birds, sea otters and harbor seals. There seems to be a lot of bald eagles in this area. Beautiful! They are so majestic, with a wingspan of 7 feet and can weigh 14 pounds.

When we left the boat, we had to climb a steep hill. All the shops were located on this hillside, and we stopped to browse in many. I am a lucky woman being married to a guy who also loves to shop and sometimes just browse.

After eating a light lunch, we visited the Bald Eagle Foundation and then returned to Skagway via the water taxi. Upon returning to town, we explored the area and discovered a waterfall (Reid Falls) and Gold Rush Cemetery. This cemetery is the burial grounds for many of the prospectors who lost their lives while crossing the Chilkoot Pass in search of gold.

The following day we visited the Klondike Gold Rush Park and took a ride on the White Pass and Yukon Route Railway. It took us into Canada along a mountainous route once taken by the prospectors heading to the Klondike Gold Field. We saw mountains, glaciers, gorges, waterfalls, tunnels, trestles and historic sites from a vintage rail car.

After returning to town, we ate lunch at The Red Onion Saloon. It was decorated in the theme of the gold rush days. After lunch, we crossed the river and strolled through the ghost town of Dyea.

119

It is where the Chilkoot Trail started and also is the location of the Slice Cemetery. In the Slice Cemetery everyone buried there died on the same day from an avalanche in 1898 along the Chilkoot Trail.

While we were in Dyea we saw mushers training their dogs with wheeled sleds. It is a beautiful area and again the bald eagles were soaring over our heads. We spotted some eagles on their nests with their young.

On our last day in Alaska I was sad. The time we had spent there left us with great memories that we will cherish forever. It was July 12th and there was much to see between Alaska and Ohio. I missed the kids and grandkids and wanted to spend some time with them before the weather turned cold and we had to leave Ohio and go south for the winter.

I wonder what it would be like to visit this land in the winter with snow and subzero temperatures, where darkness covers the land most of the day, and the Northern Lights light the sky.

My dream is to return to Alaska someday. "If you can dream it, you can do it." Would it be as exciting the second time around, probably not? I'm sure there is much we missed, and we are blessed to have seen it once.

I love the closeness that we have had with nature and God as we lived our dream in the land of the midnight sun.

Don at Welcome to Alaska sign

The Tundra Wilderness north of Fairbanks

Mountain Goats in Denali N.P

A Ride in a Wheeled Dog Sled

Don in front of Anchorage Welcome Station

Glacier at Kenai Fjords N.P.

# SEVEN

We left Skagway and traveled north on the Klondike Highway, to Rt.8 in the Yukon Territory, then east on the Alaska Highway to Watson Lake. We camped at the junction of the Alaska Highway and Rt.37. Part of Rt.8 was not paved, but it was a good road. It was a good travel day, cloudy and 60 degrees.

We stopped and had lunch at a place called Mukluk Annie's. I love the odd names of these restaurants and lodges. It makes me wonder how they came up with such names.

We arrived at camp at 5:30 pm Pacific Time and were anxious to get settled in for the night. We were fortunate enough to get the last camping space available. We continued to have snow capped mountains and tall northern pines surrounding us.

After a good night's sleep and a good breakfast, we continued down Rt.37 into British Columbia. About a third of the day's travel was on narrow gravel road with some construction and again, DUST. With many mountains and lakes, it was a beautiful ride.

Our camp for the night was at a campground located behind a lodge. We went to the lodge for dinner and I said to Don "All I want is a good hamburger." After looking at the menu I decided to order their "ground meat" sandwich. When it came it looked so good. I couldn't wait to sink my teeth into it. After taking my first bite, I knew it was not from the farm, it was not from an animal known as a cow. What was this thing I was eating? Maybe bear, elk, moose or even caribou. Whatever it was, I couldn't eat it. It had a wild, strong taste. (Lesson: when traveling in the wilderness of Canada never, ever order a ground meat sandwich unless you have a liking for those "wild things.")

For the next three days we traveled south through British Columbia heading toward the United States. It was a beautiful ride through Fraser Canyon, along the Thompson River and the Fraser River. We saw a mother bear and her two cubs along the road and many wild flowers. There seemed to be a lot of daisies, which are my favorite flower. The temperature got warmer and the hours of darkness in a day increased, as we made our way down to Highway 101 on the Pacific Coast. We crossed the U.S. border on July 18th, into the state of Washington. I hid the plants under the bed again just to be on the safe side and the border crossing went without incident.

The wilderness was behind us, which was quite apparent as the traffic increased. We had to take a 30 minute ferry ride from Keystone to Port Townsend. The cost to take our RV and Jeep was $42. I wasn't thrilled to be getting on a boat again, but the scenery was great and it was the best way to reach Highway 101.

We stopped at a place called Westport, Washington and camped on the Pacific Ocean. Near the water the temperature was much cooler.

We explored the town of Westport, visiting several little shops on the coast and then we drove through the cranberry bogs. We ended our day by driving the Jeep on the beach and having dinner downtown overlooking the harbor.

The following day we again found a campground located on the ocean, in Charleston, Oregon. The day started out sunny but by afternoon the fog rolled in with a mist. In town we went to look for seals in the harbor but saw only one.

We took a drive to Cape Arago (suggested by the locales) to view seals. The drive along the ocean was wonderful. The fog lifted and, as we drove high on a cliff above the surf, we could hear the seals barking but could not see any. All was not lost; we did witness a spectacular sunset and returned to camp feeling tired and blessed.

Entering California was a bit more complicated than crossing the U.S.-Canadian border. We came to the border and a border guard stopped us and entered the RV. I thought, "Oh no, there goes my beloved plants." He asked us some questions about transporting fruit. I haven't seen any good fruit for quite some time. "No, we have no fruit" we said, "We sure would like some." He was not a pleasant man and continued to look around the camper and in the refrigerator. After a few more questions we were again on our way. My plants were safe again.

Our next stop was in the Redwood National Forest along the coast of Northern California. The redwood trees are the tallest and oldest trees in the world. They range from 200 to over 350 feet tall and live up to 2000 years. These tall trees make the RV look small.

We camped at the mouth of the Klamath River, and after setting up camp we took a coastal drive through the redwoods. We saw whales spouting in the sea and seals sunning on the rocks. The road was high on a bluff overlooking the Pacific. Breathtaking! We stopped at the Big Tree (a tree that stands out in this forest). It is 304 feet tall and 21 feet in diameter.

Then we hiked the Fern Canyon Trail. It was a nice loop trail with several different kinds of fern covering the canyon walls like a thick carpet.

The following day we drove through the famous 700 year old redwoods, then had lunch at the Forest Cafe.

Our next adventure was a four hour tour jet boat ride on the Klamath River. We saw osprey and bald eagle and stopped up the river at a lodge for dinner. Steak, fruit, salad and wine. We both enjoyed this adventure and thought it was well worth the cost.

We continued down Highway 101 (Avenues of the Giants), thirty-one miles of redwood groves. We saw the Immortal Tree, Eternal Tree House and Chimney Tree. It made us feel so small among these huge trees.

Next we took Route 101 to Route 1. This was a very winding, narrow, mountain road. We had several stuffed animals on our bed. A black bear (Clyde) from the Smoky Mountains, a moose (Harvey) from Minnesota, a polar bear (Ernie) from Alaska and a puffin bird (Peter) also from

Alaska. We knew it had been a rough day when we looked back on the bed and Peter Puffin was gone. This was one of those days.

We traveled south through the Sonoma Wine Country and then on to San Francisco. July 30th and the temperature was 100 degrees. It was not a good day to be in the city. We stopped to watch a kite festival on a hillside on our way into the city. What a wondrous sight to see so many beautiful kites filling the sky, all shapes and sizes and very bright colors.

Once in the city we walked to pier 39 and went in a few shops, had lunch and then walked to fisherman's wharf. We attempted to get tickets for the ferry to Alcatraz but they were sold out for the next week. It was too hot to enjoy the day.

The following day it was 105 degrees. I didn't like the extreme heat. We took a ride through Napa Valley and stopped to taste a few wines. We tried to stay in the air conditioning as much as possible. We returned to camp and headed for the pool.

Catching Our Dreams

By the first of August I was anxious to head east and see family. Living in an RV full time is great but I was starting to get homesick, even without a home to go to. I miss the summer months in Ohio, the fresh fruits and vegetables right from the garden, family picnics, spending time with my friends and going to grandkids' sport events.

Our next stop was Reno, Nevada. Don again felt very blessed. We arrived just in time for a custom car show called "Hot August Nights." People lined the streets with chairs as if waiting for a parade.

The cars that cruised up and down the streets were from the 1960"s (our teenage years). The loudspeakers blasted music from the same era. We had a great time and dream of someday returning for another "Hot August Night."

As the evening came to an end, the sky became very dark and cloudy as if it might storm. It didn't rain but there was a lighting strike, in the foothills around Reno, causing some ground fires. You could see the fires in the distance.

In the morning, when we awoke, there were ashes on our car and RV. Several homes were threatened and evacuated but none were destroyed. Even though it was far in the distance, it was a very scary sight to see the night sky lit up by fire.

We continued our journey east traveling Route 50 across Nevada. Rt.50 is often referred to as "The Loneliest Road in America." We crossed miles and miles of desert and saw miles and miles of sage.

As we approached the town of Ely, the location of our next night's stop, we could see smoke filling the skies over the desert. The closer we came to town the thicker the smoke became. It was burning our throats and causing our eyes to water. It was worse than driving through a thick fog. It was only 5 in the afternoon, but it was pitch black outside. We couldn't see two feet in front of us. A policeman appeared and escorted us through. We could only see the taillights of the police cruiser as we crept along. Apparently lightning struck an area west of the town the day before and the sage was still burning. To this day, when I think back to that day in the desert, I can still smell that awful smell of the thick black smoke.

We again entered the state of Utah. It is one of my favorite states to visit, especially the eastern part, with the magnificent red rock formations. We stayed in a town called Green River. The temperature continued to be 100 degrees, too hot to enjoy almost anything.

We spent the following day in the camper in the air conditioning. Don watched a race on TV and I went stir crazy, cooped up in this small area with the TV blaring. O.K. I admit this lifestyle can get to you when you have several HOT days in a row. I long for some large shade trees and a nice cool breeze. I long for Ohio. The following day was the same, with temperatures in the 100s and again we stayed inside and tried to stay cool and entertained.

By the third day we were ready to move on. We began the day with a pancake breakfast provided by the camp host. Yummy! Then we were on the road headed toward Denver. Don wanted to visit the Sports Car Club of America National

Headquarters. He wanted to buy some books, stickers, etc. We got off Rt.25 to get gas.

As we turned the corner the coffee cup fell out of it's holder and spilled coffee on the carpet. And if that's not enough, a police cruiser was behind us with his lights flashing. "What did you do?" I ask. "I don't know, but if he thinks I can just pull this long thing over along this busy highway he is mistaken." he answered. We continued to the next traffic light and turned into the gas station. After all, gas is the reason we got off our route in the first place.

When Don gets nervous he chuckles. I don't mean he breaks down and goes into hysterics, but he has a nervous chuckle and a grin on his face (his mom does the same thing when she's nervous). So here we were pulled up to the gas pump with the police cruiser behind us, lights flashing. Don got out of the motor home with a grin on his face. Needless to say, the policeman is not a happy camper, but Don is, smiling from ear to ear. Don said through his smile and a few chuckles, "What's the problem officer? Do you mind if I fill up the tank while we talk? Ha,Ha."

At this point I am picturing the policeman hauling Don, the happy one, off to jail. I would have to drive this home of ours to camp alone. Please Don just do what the nice, not too happy, policeman says. He makes Don wait to fill the RV with gas while he writes him out a ticket for not using his turn signal when he turned off the highway. Then he gave him a lecture about stopping when he first put on his flashers. Don tried to explain that he needed a large area to get the RV and Jeep off the road. I think the officer got tired of my husband's happy face and returned to his cruiser and took off. We were lucky. We got away with just a ticket. If we would have had to appear in court, the judge would have locked this happy man up and threw away the key.

We continued our journey east through the cornfields of Nebraska. The heat wave continued the next few days. The large windshield of the RV is great for sightseeing but the vastness of it lets in a lot of heat on the very hot days. The dash air does very little to cool off the large space in our home. We turned on the generator while we were driving and ran the central air. This helped to cool things down but it doesn't help our gas mileage much, at 102 degrees we didn't really care. We were so tired of being hot.

We stopped in Hannibal, Missouri and camped at Injun Joe's Campground. We spent the following day touring Hannibal and took a stern wheel boat ride down the Mississippi River. The temperature was in the 80's and we were at last enjoying the slightly cooler weather.

We continued onward through Illinois and then into Indiana. We stayed in Indianapolis a few days and went to the Indiana State Fair, attended an auto race at the Indianapolis Raceway Park and toured the nearby town of Metamora.

Metamora is a historic canal town. A relaxing way to spend a beautiful summer day exploring its shops, cafes and taking a canal boat ride pulled by giant draft horses. The evenings were cool and we had to dig out our sweatshirts.

On August 20th we arrived home.

Driving the Dreamcatcher through the
Redwoods Of California

Sandy in a redwood tree

# EIGHT

After six months on the road we were once again in Ohio. It felt strange not to have a home to return to. It seemed as if we had been on a very long vacation.

After trying a few area parks we settled on a place called Clay's Park. It is located in an area near our family. The park has a nice swimming lake, water slides, paddle boats, indoor pool, miniature golf, hayrides, weekend entertainment and Sunday church service. It was a great place to have fun and enjoy a few months with our kids and grandkids, (Chris 11, Vinnie 11, Alex 8, Lindsay 8, Brandon 3, Brady 2 and Brooke 1). They had all grown so much in six months.

We stayed at Clay's park until November 1st when they closed for the winter. We moved in with my dad for the month of November, and stored the RV at a nearby lot. My dad was turning 90 on November 17th and I couldn't miss the big celebration. We had dinner at a restaurant and had a family gathering at my sister, Sharon's house to celebrate. It was a hot time. The cake had 90 lit candles. Whew! I love getting together with family and family gatherings were what I missed most while we were on the road.

But by the end of November, the days were getting cold and we were ready to start heading south.

We left dad's house on November 25th and traveled straight south. It rained most of the day and it was cold and miserable. We decided to spend the night in a motel. We had no water in the RV and most campgrounds were closed. We traveled 456 miles and when we stopped for the night, it didn't take long for us to fall asleep.

Our destination for this journey was the Southwest. Like all our travels, we first started out with a visit to Don's parents. We had not spent Christmas with them for several years and were looking forward to spending the holidays in Texas.

We stopped at a park in Benton, Arkansas on our second night. It was great to be back in the Dreamcatcher and in our own bed. The temperature was in the 60's and dropped into the 40's that night, but we were warm and cozy in our home.

I called my dad that evening. "Hi dad," I said "we're in Arkansas." "Well, I'm going on vacation." he replied. "Where are you going?" I ask. "I'm going to Florida with your brother." he said. "Great, you need to go where it is warm." I commented. "I won't be home if you call." He sounded so happy and I am so grateful he could go. He loves to travel as much as we do. I told him our plans to spend the holiday with Don's parents and told him to enjoy his vacation. This love for travel is in my genes, I am sure.

We arrived in Texas and stayed along the Gulf Coast. The camp was called Serendipity Resort and Marina, located on the shores of the Gulf of Mexico. How strange it seemed to be looking out over the ocean knowing that my dad was in Clearwater, Florida on the other side of this huge body of water.

We continued south about 100 miles to Pioneer RV Park and Resort in Port Aransas, Texas. It is located on the north end of Mustang Island near Corpus Christi. It is nestled in the middle of sand dunes. This was a great camp to stay awhile and do what we love best, explore.

It was November 28th and 80 degrees. We were again wearing shorts, and loving this life style. First thing we did was climb the sand dunes and walk on the beautiful beach. There was a warm breeze coming off the ocean. The water was a turquoise blue and the sand a white powder. After soaking up some much needed sun, we drove into the town of Port Aransas We learned that Mustang Island is noted for its many birding sites and has the highest bird count on the Gulf Coast. While we were in town we visited the Leona Belie Turnbull Birding Center and saw many birds and wildlife including an alligator.

We stayed at Pioneer Park a week. While we were there, we visited the U.S.S. Lexington Aircraft Carrier and the Texas State Aquarium. With the sides and top off our jeep, we took a drive south to Padre Island National Seashore. Having a Jeep is the greatest. After about 6 miles the road ended. Just because the road ended didn't mean we had to stop. We turned onto the beach and drove another 20 miles south. We watched the waves break and saw many birds. We watched the dolphins swimming in the surf while we were basking in the sun. A perfect day.

Our next stop was further south on South Padre Island. We stayed at the county park located on the beach. To help us get into the Christmas spirit, which was hard to do in the 80 degrees heat, we attended a night time Electric Christmas Parade. It was fantastic. The floats were lit with colored lights and were made in beach themed shapes such as ships, fish, lighthouses and sand castles. The lights on the floats lit up the night sky and created a magical, seasonal atmosphere.

We arrived at Don's parent's house on December 9th just in time to help set up their Christmas tree. We stayed at the same RV park as we did the year before, and celebrated Christmas and New Years with them and their friends.

In January our daughter, Debbie called and said she wanted to come to Texas to see us and her grandparents. She arranged a flight into San Antonio. We love San Antonio and agreed to meet her at the airport and spend the day touring the city. Seeing her was great.

We toured the Alamo, which is located right in the middle of this large city. (It looks a bit out of place among the modern buildings). The battle of the Alamo was fought in 1836. A walk through this old mission was awesome.

In the evening we went to the River Walk, which is lined with many shops, bars and restaurants. We had dinner on the river and enjoyed the impressive festival of lights that was displayed during the Christmas season.

After spending the night in a motel we returned to Mission the following day. The ride took five hours through the flattest and most barren land we have traveled. No trees, no grass, no buildings for as far as our eyes could see, just flat land with sagebrush and cactus.

We enjoyed the time spent with our daughter, dinning out, visiting Mexico, and even taking a day trip to South Padre Island where we rode horses on the beach. Debbie at the time owned her own horse and was used to riding, but Don and I were not. After a short ride we were ready to get off our horses, but she was ready to run. Needless to say by the end of the ride we had trouble walking. Oh, what we do for our kids. Time went by way too fast and it was time for Debbie to return to Ohio, and for us to return to our travels. The memories of her visit will last us a lifetime.

We once again said our goodbyes to my in-laws and were on our way across Texas, New Mexico and came to a stop in Arizona. We stayed in Tucson and visited San Xavier Mission. Organ pipe Cactus National Monument and Saguaro National Park.

San Xavier Mission, nicknamed "White Dove in the Desert", is a Historic Catholic Mission south of Tucson founded in 1699 and is a striking sight to see. It stands out in this flat desert and as we toured this magnificent church we were in awe of its beauty.

Next, we visited Organ Pipe Cactus National Monument. It is located on the Mexican border in the Sonoran Desert. As we drove through the park, we were struck by the desert wilderness. It is the opposite of the wilderness of the north, where there were tall pines and thick forest. Here there was nothing but desert and sand and tall cacti. Completely different, but the same in the fact that there was no civilization and we again had the feeling of being the only two people on earth. The organ pipe cactus grows between 15 and 20 feet tall and the Sonoran Desert is the only place in the U.S. where they grow wild. As we toured this park, getting out of the Jeep and taking pictures, we marveled at this magnificent cactus and the beautiful preservation of the American Southwest. Don tried his best to find a Gila monster (a venomous lizard), but had no success. Why is this man always looking for strange wildlife?

Next on our list of places to see was the Saguaro National Park. It is the home of the world's largest cacti. The Giant Saguaro is the universal symbol of the American west. It is native to Sonora Desert and can grow up to 70 feet tall. It is a tree like cactus with branches (or arms) and all the arms point upward. While in the park we took a few short trails and Don was still looking for a Gila monster, instead we saw a beautiful rainbow. This was more to my liking.

No trip to the Southwest would be complete without a visit to Tombstone, Arizona. It is the most authentic western town left in the United States. We enjoyed walking the streets, and felt that we were back 130 years ago, with wooden sidewalk and saloons. We almost expected to see the Earp brothers around the next corner, or maybe Doc. Holiday. The most popular spot to visit is Boot Hill Cemetery. One marker we saw read "Here Lies Lester Moore, Four Slugs from a 44, No Les No More." We enjoyed our day in this well preserved frontier town.

We then continued up Route 10 toward Phoenix. The day was cloudy and warm. Along the highway was a sign that read "High Wind Area."

147

"What does that mean?" I ask. "I'm not sure." Don replied. Shortly after that a gust of wind came along and moved the entire motor home with the attached Jeep to the lane left of us. Thankfully there was no one beside us. "Now that was a very moving experience." He replied. It certainly was.

We planned to stay for a month at our next camp. The name of the town was Casa Grande. It is located between Phoenix and Tucson. There was so much to see in this area and we needed a break from being on the road. Casa Grande was named after the Hohokam Indian Ruins at nearby Casa Grande National Monument.

We would wake every day to a bright sunny sky. After having a good breakfast, we would either walk or ride our bikes on a nearby desert trail. Each day there was a new adventure awaiting us. We went to visit the Casa Grande National Monument, explored the arid desert, saw prairie dogs, attended Indian Days, went to an Indian Pow Wow, and went to a rodeo This was a great town and we enjoyed everything it had to offer.

While staying at Casa Grande we frequently took day trips into Phoenix. One of the most memorable adventures was a day on the Apache Trail. It is definitely a tourist attraction, but one worth taking.

The trail was originally used by the Apache Indian to move through the Superstition Mountains, then as a stagecoach route. It is one of the most scenic drives I have ever traveled. There are canyons, geologic formations, desert plants and trees, views of lakes and wildflowers, and breathtaking desert vistas.

We started out with a full tank of gas and lots of drinking water and snacks. It is less than 50 miles long of which 22 miles are unpaved. It is not for nervous drivers and definitely not for nervous passengers. The trail can take anywhere from 2 to 7 hours depending on how many stops you make. Most of the road has a maximum speed of 15mph.

We began the trail at the town of Tortilla Flat, which has 6 inhabitants. It has one restaurant and we went in for lunch. It was called Superstition Saloon. The bar had stools with saddles for seats.

The walls were covered with dollar bills, from around the world, signed by those passing through. The original restaurant burnt down in the late 1980's and all the bills on the walls went with it. It appeared to me that the walls were again almost full of bills.

There were a few miles of payment beyond Tortilla Flat, then plenty of hairpin turns and switchbacks. I was glad I was not driving because on this road you had to keep your eyes on the road and not on the scenery. We stopped at a rest area and climbed a steep trail up a mountain to an Indian cliff dwelling. We were out of breath but in awe of the true beauty of Arizona. We returned to camp late, but we both agreed it was a great adventure.

We received a call from my brother, Bob. He and my sister-in-law, Janet wanted to fly out to visit us and bring my dad. I said "Sure come ahead, we would love to see you." Of course when they got there we had a cold spell but that didn't stop us from having a good time. We had a week together visiting and we took them to many places we had visited including the Apache Trail. Dad kept saying "I don't believe all of this." He was so amazed and enjoyed all that nature had to offer. Janet and Don combed the desert floor for geos and found a few; they also found some beautiful rocks.

We took a day and visited the Arizona-Sonora Desert Museum in Tucson. It is a zoo, natural history museum and botanical garden all in one. It was all outside with a lot of walking so we had dad sit in a wheelchair and he seemed to enjoy it without getting tired. The week passed quickly and it was time for them to return home. I am so grateful for the memories that this time has given us.

Soon after dad left we received a call from our son, Brian. He was going on vacation with his family to Las Vegas. "Hey mom." He said. "Can you meet us for a visit in Vegas?" We love these visits from family. It keeps us from being homesick. "Sure, we can." I replied.

Before we left Casa Grande we found some tickets, in a newspaper ad, for Las Vegas Motor Speedway to see a NASCAR Race. I called Brian to see if he would want to go. Of course he did. The auto racing fever is in his blood too. Don spent the next weekend volunteering at the Phoenix racetrack, and then we were once again on the road, heading toward Vegas.

After looking in the Trailer Life Camping Guide, to find a place to park the Dreamcatcher, we decided to stay at Sam's Town RV Park and Casino. It was a very nice place about 3 miles east of the strip. We had a great time with Brian and his family and especially with our two year old granddaughter, Brooke. We went swimming at our campground pool, shopped in the casinos and attended a very exciting NASCAR Race, that even I enjoyed. We kept busy and the week flew by as it seems to do when we are with family,

Our next stop was Yuma, Arizona where the sun shines 95% of the time, the sky is blue and the humidity is low. It was just the place to be in early March.

While we were there we took an off the road ride in our Jeep. We had a map, so how could we get lost? Did you ever try to follow a map through a desert? We started out on a dirt road off the highway. Twisting and turning. After awhile it was hard to tell the dirt road from the dry river beds. We kept driving and driving and driving. The desert scenery was wonderful. Desert flowers in bloom, cacti, sagebrush and not a soul for as far as we could see. Our map showed the dirt road would come out on a main highway, but it was getting late and we had no clue if we were still on a road or just a washed out creek bed. We didn't know exactly where we were or which way we should go.

Finally we spotted some trucks off in the distance. We drove toward them hoping they could help us find our way out of this desolate place. Don got out of the Jeep and approached the two men standing beside their truck. Just then a third man came out of a hole in the ground. "Can you help us please; we can't seem to find our way out of this desert." "Just a minute," the man replied. "Fire in the hole," he yelled. Just then a big "BOOM" shook the earth beneath us. The three men were laughing. "What was that?" Don yelled. "Dynamite," he said. "We're mining." "Well it scared the bejeebers out of me," was Don's response. When they were all done laughing, at our expense, they told us to turn around and go back the way we came. Now if we could just remember the way we came. We made it back to the Dreamcatcher about dark. We were tired and hungry, but thankful to be home.

While we were in Yuma we visited the Yuma Territorial Prison. It was in operation from 1876 to 1909. The cells were small and the prisoners had been chained to the floor. In over three decades there were 3069 prisoners of which 29 were women. While we were there, Don took my "mug shot" behind a cell door. I am glad that I only had to stand in the cell for a few minutes. I am not one to be confined. From Yuma we also took a day trip to Algodones, Mexico and enjoyed an authentic Mexican meal.

At the beginning of March we have two grandsons with birthdays on the same day. Brandy was turning 3 and Brandon was turning 4. I did what any grandma would do; I sent them both a card and some money to buy a desired toy. We also called them on their birthdays to make sure they received their cards and to wish them a "Happy Birthday." "Grandma," Brandon said in a very sad voice "you forgot my birthday." "I didn't forget. Did you get the card?" I asked. "Yes" he said. "But you didn't come to my party." He sounded almost in tears. He didn't understand how far away we were. To this day I feel sad when I think of how we disappointed our grandsons. This lifestyle is somewhat a selfish way to live, and I was not sure how much longer I wanted to continue our adventure.

We left Yuma and drove toward Los Angeles, California. We camped at a private park outside the city, taking several day trips by Jeep. We went to Disneyland, where Don had his picture taken with his favorite character, Donald Duck. We visited the La Brea Tar Pits, amazing. Went for a ride on Mulholland Drive for a fabulous view of L.A. Took a guided tour of movie stars' homes, and walked some of the famous streets of the city. We also took a day trip down the Pacific Coast to the town of La Jolla, where we saw several sea lions sunbathing on the beach.

The coastline of California has a beauty all its own. It is a place where nature seems to awaken all your senses, the smell and taste of the salty air, the feel of the wind in your hair, the sight of huge rocks off shore, and the sound of the endless roar of the waves. I don't know how the dangerous sea, with high winds and large crashing waves, can have such a calming effect on me, but it does. What a beautiful world we live in.

Our next destination was inland to Sequoia National Park in central California. The park is famous for its giant sequoia trees in a beautiful section of the Sierra Nevada Mountains. We took a trail to the General Sherman Tree, one of the largest trees on earth and Tunnel Log, which has a tunnel cut through a fallen giant sequoia tree. The trees were beautiful and since we were in a high elevation there was snow on the ground, yet we were plenty warm hiking in sweat shirts.

The roads were dry, but snow was visible all around us. It seemed to cling to every branch of the tall trees. It was so peaceful traveling on these roads through the park and it reminded me of winters in Ohio. The quiet and stillness of new fallen snow creates a peace and calm within my soul.

While we were in California, Don wanted to visit and work at some of the sport car tracks he had read about. Thunderhill in Willow, Sears Point in Sonoma and Laguna Seca in Salinas. We decided to go north up the middle of the state and begin this tour of race tracks, at Thunderhill Raceway.

The middle of California is farming communities, with miles of fruit orchards, fields of vegetables, and farmland. This scenery reminds me of the farmlands at home. Everything looked so green.

We passed several roadside markets and decided to stop at one. "Let's buy an artichoke," Don said. "I don't even know how to cook an artichoke" I replied. "Well we'll ask the cashier, she looks like a good cook" he said. He proceeded to ask the cashier and she handed him a pamphlet

157

on artichokes. It must be a question that is commonly asked. The pamphlet was titled "How to cook and eat an artichoke." You need a lesson on eating one of these strange looking vegetables? I am used to eating peas, beans and corn. I don't remember needing a lesson to learn to eat any of the Ohio grown veggies. O.K. we will give them a try when we get to camp. We cooked them, and ate them, but I did not like them. Maybe there is a better way to cook artichoke.

We continued north until we came to Shasta National Forest and stopped at a place called McArthur Burney Falls Memorial State Park. We set up camp and decided we would go for a hike to see what every other camper was describing as the most beautiful falls in California.

We started out at the visitors' center and decided to take one of the three trails leading to the falls. The trail wound through the park's evergreen forest and across a bridge. There it was. The beautiful, 129 foot Burney Falls. We were at the bottom of the falls looking up. It was truly beautiful. The water fell to the creek below and large rocks were in and near the water. We sat on a rock and were in awe of its sound and beauty. We are blessed to have seen so much of God's creation.

After a long rest, we started back to the visitors' center. I was in front of Don, walking along, looking everywhere except where I was going. Don yelled "Sandy stop, don't move." I stopped dead in my tracks. I could tell there was fear in his words. He said "slowly back up towards me." I looked down and in front of me, stretched across the path, was a rattle snake. Don said it was about 3 or 4 feet long, but as time goes by, like many fish stories, the length of that snake has grown larger. I backed up to a safe distance and my "Knight in Shining Armor" went to battle for my safety. He picked up a rock and threw it at the snake. The snake started to rattle. We backed up some more. There was a couple coming down the trail from the opposite direction. Don yelled and warned them of the snake. We all waited for the snake to calm down and finally he moved on. (Lesson: never throw a rock at a rattle snake).

159

We arrived just in time for the weekend race in Willow, Calf. Don enjoyed his time working at Thunderhill, while I had a relaxing time around town and at the campground.

Our next stop was Sears Point Race Track located just north of San Francisco. During our week there, we spent an afternoon in Chinatown. San Francisco is anything but flat and by the time we were finished with our walking tour we were both tired.

Don worked the track at Sears Point, then we traveled south to the last race track on our list, located near Monterey. We camped at a county park that was located on a hill overlooking the racetrack. It was a nice wooded park and the view from our camper was Laguna Seca Raceway, which Don found to be almost heaven. We walked around the campground and met the camp hosts. They were also full timers.

Some government owned campgrounds give free camping to the camp host in exchange for work. This host and her husband were required to work 20 hours a week. This is one way to help with the expenses of living this lifestyle. In our travels we also met couples who would work a chain store in the north in the summer and transfer with the same store to the south in the winter. Some work odd jobs or sell their crafts or even write books to help with the cost.

As night drew near we entered the Dreamcatcher to watch a movie on TV. All at once, with alarm in his voice Don yells "What was that?" "What was what?" I was almost afraid to ask. "I think I just saw a mouse run out from under the dash board." he said. "Where did he go?" I yelled. "Back under the dash" he replied. Well now, I'm not about to share our motor home with a mouse. I wouldn't be able to sleep with the knowledge of a rodent in our home. "I'll go tomorrow and buy a trap" he said.

Suddenly I remember a note I received from one of my favorite patients before I retired. It was from an elderly lady named Mary. Mary said in the note that she envied us of our journey across America. She also gave me the advice to not forget to look up. You will miss a lot if you don't look up, she wrote. She ended the note by saying not to be surprised if at some point in our journey we see a mouse in our motor home. It would be her traveling with us. "No trap" I yelled. "You can't kill Mary!" "You named the mouse?" he said laughing. I proceeded to tell him about the note from Mary.

After giving it much thought we decided to try to trap "Mary" in our small cooler with a flip top lid. We placed a cracker with peanut butter on it in the cooler and laid the cooler on its side. We propped the lid open with Don's shoe and waited. The plan was to wait until the mouse was in the cooler then kick the shoe and the lid would close trapping "Mary" inside. We didn't have to wait long. "Mary" came out to get her lunch but she was much faster than we were and we missed.

On our second attempt we stationed ourselves farther away from the cooler and used a long stick to knock the shoe from holding the lid open and this time our plan worked. "Mary" was in the cooler. We carried it outside and laid the cooler on its side. Opening the lid we waited but she didn't come out. Looking inside was "Mary" looking very content. We shook the cooler and she finally came out and looked at us as if to say "how can you do this to me?' I felt bad, but I knew I couldn't live with a mouse in my house.

We had the week to explore the area before Don was to work the race. We took several day trips to the Pacific Coast. We visited Monterey Bay and watched the sea otters play in the surf. They lay on their backs and break open shells by hitting them with a rock to dislodge its prey. They look very lazy as they float and bob up and down with the waves.

Our visit to Monterey Bay Aquarium, which is perched on the edge of the Pacific in Cannery Row, was well worth the time. Our oceans hold an incredible variety of God's creatures, some of which I will only see in an aquarium. The part of the earth in which we live, is such a very small part of this wondrous world, how lucky we are to get a peek at life beyond our own backyard.

We drove the Big Sur Coastline and the notorious 17 mile drive. This section of Highway 1 is considered one of the most scenic driving routes in America. It is where the Santa Lucia Mountains rise abruptly from the Pacific Ocean. The highway winds along the western flank of the mountains varying from near sea level up to a thousand feet drop to the water. The views from this drive were stunning.

Spending the day in the town of Pacific Groves was relaxing and worthwhile. It is nicknamed "Butterfly Town U.S.A." It is known for its Victorian Homes and the migration of the Monarch butterfly. It would be quite a sight to see all those butterflies in one place. Unfortunately, they had left a month before we arrived, a definite place to return to in late February or March.

We went to Lovers Point Beach Park and ate a picnic lunch and were in awe of the beauty of this place. Surfers were in the water riding the waves; the coast was lined with beautiful purple flowers for as far as the eye could see. The park was clean and families were playing in the grassy areas. We spent the day walking the cement path along the coast and enjoying every minute, stopping on the occasional park bench to sit and DREAM.

The weekend came and Don worked the race at Laguna Seca Raceway Park. We packed the Dreamcatcher and left the County Park and headed east, leaving behind "Mary" and the beautiful Pacific Coast.

Our next stop was Yosemite National Park. Yosemite is one of the first wilderness parks in the U.S. and is known for its waterfalls. It also has deep valleys, green meadows, ancient sequoias and a wilderness area. We hiked some of the trails and saw El Capitan, a prominent granite cliff that looms over Yosemite Valley. My favorite view was that of Yosemite Falls. It is 2,425 feet high and is the highest falls in North America. The scenery in this park was outstanding and we enjoyed again the wonders of nature.

As we continued east I was getting anxious to see our family and friends. We are beginning to feel cramped in our small home, with so little space to call our own. As we were driving the back roads of this wondrous country we saw people mowing lawns and playing in their yards. I long for a home with a garden. A house with a long front porch with a porch swing, and a view of the rolling hills and farmlands of Ohio. I miss having a church home and meeting friends for lunch. This life we have been living was great for awhile but now we are beginning to start a new dream. A dream of finding a lot and building a house, but like all dreams it will take a lot of planning. We already know "IF YOU CAN DREAM IT, YOU CAN DO IT."

As we continued east, we traveled across Utah and stopped to see Sundance Resort. We rode the chair lift to the top of a mountain and hiked a trail back down. It was a sunny day and we could see for miles from the lift. We could also see Robert Redford's Ranch off in the distance. He sure lives in a beautiful area.

We spent a few days in Rocky Mountain National Park in Colorado, with snowcapped mountains and crystal clear lakes, wooded forest and mountain tundra. We saw elk, moose and bighorn sheep and the majestic mountain views were outstanding.

It was then May, and I couldn't seem to get home fast enough. I wanted to spend the summer with family and friends. We wanted to make a few more stops and hoped to be home by the first part of June.

Driving through South Dakota we stopped to see the Crazy Horse Monument. It is a mountain carving that was under construction on privately held land in the Black Hills. It depicts Crazy Horse, an Oglala Lakota warrior riding a horse and pointing into the distance. It was being carved out of Thunderhead Mountain and when completed will measure 641 ft, wide and 563 ft. high. It has been in progress since 1948. Wow, now that's amazing.

Seventeen miles down the road we stopped to see another mountain carving, Mount Rushmore National Monument, another awesome sight. It features 60 ft. sculptures of the heads of four U.S. presidents, George Washington, Thomas Jefferson, Theodore Roosevelt, and Abraham Lincoln,

167

representing the first 130 years of the United States.

We spent a day exploring the Badlands National Park. After viewing the land from a high point we could definitely understand the name Badlands. It was a very rugged terrain with an almost moonlike landscape. Millions of years of wind, water and erosion chiseled spires, deep canyons and jagged buttes. After a stop at the visitors' center, we discovered there was much more to this wonderful place.

We took a loop driving tour and discovered not only the ruggedness of the park, but also the grasslands. We saw buffalo grazing and could almost feel the American Indian spirit with us. It was great to see this land preserved and untouched by modern man. During our drive we also saw prairie dog towns with their cute heads popping up everywhere.

A few stopped cars ahead told us there was something worth seeing. As we approached we saw several wild donkeys. I rolled down my window and held out a cracker to a sweet looking donkey.

He stuck his whole head in the window and I thought he was also going to eat me. We finally got out of the car and the donkeys crowded around us. They were looking for more handouts. It was a great way to end our trip for the year.

As we headed further east we made few stops and arrived home the second week of June.

Riding horses on the beach at South Padre Island

Dad and Sandy in Arizona desert

Sandy beside an organ pipe cactus

Lost in the Yuma desert

171

Pacific Groves, California

Wild Donkeys in the Badlands

# NINE

Arriving home we parked the Dreamcatcher at Clay's Park, where we had parked the previous summer. My family had a welcome home picnic for us and it was great seeing everyone. Our children and grandchildren spent time with us at the park, even putting up their own tents and spending the night. We had a great time swimming, paddle boating, and roasting marshmallows around the campfire. I missed being with family and playing with the grandkids. We also had a couple of our friends over for dinner and spent an evening around the fire.

When you are traveling full time you don't stay in one place long enough to form a close friendship. It's been a great adventure but we are beginning to realize there is much that we miss.

While we were home, Don had a chance to race his car a few times at local sports car tracks. He would get up early in the morning and drive to the track with his race car in tow.

One weekend when he was racing, our three grandsons, Alex, Brandon, and Brady were spending the night. They were excited and had a hard time falling asleep. Finally they were sleeping and we went to bed. Don's alarm went off at 4:30am. The boys slept through the alarm, thank goodness and they slept through what happened next.

As Don stepped out the door, he was expecting to step down two steps to the ground. Instead he took one big giant leap to the ground because someone had pushed the switch that raised the steps.

I'm not sure which one of the boys did it, but I'm guessing it was our 3yr. old grandson, Brady, who was forever pushing buttons and switches to see what would happen.

Don was not a bit happy at the time, but looking back we laugh at that episode. Sometimes the surprises in our life, even the ones that seem bad at the time, turn out to be some of our best memories.

In July the park celebrated "Christmas in July". Dad came out to spend the day at the camper and spent some time talking to Santa. We enjoyed being with Dad so much, he could make a boring day fun. I felt time passing quickly and again realized the time we spend with loved ones is gone too fast.

If we were going to make the dream of building a house come true, we had to first find the perfect lot. It needed to be in the country and have a great view.

We spent many hours driving the back roads and searching for just the right location. Finally we found some lots south of the city of Wooster, Ohio. It was a soybean field divided into several 1 1/2 acre lots. We drove the Jeep to the middle of a few of the lots to help us decide on the best view. Finally, we made a decision. The one we chose was across from a small farm with a white barn. A few horses were grazing in the pasture directly across from our chosen lot. We walked the land and I found the exact spot that I wanted our porch swing to hang.

From my future porch, I could see the pasture, and beyond, rolling hills and farmland. What a spectacular view. The land sat up on a hill, I said to Don "This is it." He agreed it was just what we had been looking for.

We purchased the lot and knew we would not start to build right away. We had no idea the kind of house we wanted or who would build it. This would take a lot of serious thought.

In the meantime we wanted to build a pole barn to hold the things we were storing in a rented storage unit. At the time we were paying $100 a month to rent space to store the race car, tools and the few antiques we couldn't give up.

A friend of our daughter worked in construction and agreed to build the 24x40 foot building in the back of our lot. By the end of summer it was completed and our belongings were safely stored inside.

In August we celebrated our grandson Alex's 10th birthday and watched a few of his football games. We attended a Labor Day picnic at our daughter's house with all the children and grandchildren, playing games and eating a great feast. The following day we attended another picnic at a nearby park with my aunts, cousins, dad, brothers and sisters and their families.

Family and friends is certainly what life is all about. I love to travel, but I also enjoy coming home and spending time with the most important people in the world to me.

After being away for two years, it was time to make appointments for all our annual checkups with our doctors and dentist. On a beautiful September morning I was sitting in the eye doctor's waiting room waiting for Don to come out of the office. I was glancing at a magazine and half listening to a TV that was on. The events that happened next had us and the entire country in shock. The terrorist attacks of 9/11/2001 unfolded right in front of our eyes.

How could this be happening to our beloved America? As most Americans, that day and for several days and weeks following, we prayed for the victims and watched this tragic event unfold. The battle against terrorism would never be over and our lives would be changed forever. I believe home should be a place you feel safe. Has this changed? I sincerely hope not or the terrorists win.

As fall approaches, and the leaves start to turn color and fall, it is the best and most beautiful time of the year to visit my sister Maxine and her husband Ralph, in the Finger Lake Region of New York. They live on Keuka Lake and were the owners of the Hammondsport Motel. I called dad and asked if he wanted to go with us to see Maxine. He was packed and ready to go in the blink of an eye. Always ready to go any place, any time. My sister Sharon also wanted to go, so the four of us went for a great three day weekend.

This area of the country is so beautiful in the fall with the hillsides bursting with color.

The vineyards that surround the lake had recently been picked and a few of the grapes remained on the vine. To our dad, this meant they were ours for the taking, to pick and eat straight from the vines, yummy.

We enjoyed our visit and the motel room, as usual, was nice, clean and the right price. We thanked our host and hostess and returned home to prepare for our next trip in the Dreamcatcher.

The park that we had spent the summer in closed on November 1st. After celebrating Halloween with the grandkids we headed south. Our destination was southern Florida, enough south that we would stay warm over the winter.

On our way south, we stopped and visited the city of Savannah, Georgia. Walking the historic part of the city made us feel like we had gone back in time. The streets were made of cobblestone and the old brick buildings had Spanish moss growing on them. The lights along the streets were gas lamps and flickered as we passed.

There was a cemetery in the middle of town called Colonial Park Cemetery. Savannah is noted for its many haunted tales and this cemetery is a popular stop for a walking ghost tour at night. Walking through any cemetery at night is not my cup of tea, but we did enjoy a daytime stroll, reading the historic tombstones as we walked.

Next we visited the River Street District. It's an area along the Savannah River that has an array of bars, restaurants, shops and nightclubs. Its streets are also cobblestone and there were horse drawn carriages carrying tourists on this, car forbidden street. The store clerks were in colonial dress and again I felt that I was back in time.

Tybee Island is across the river from Savannah, and we were able to spend some time on the beach, climbed a lighthouse, and explored the historic Fort Screven. Savannah has so much to do and see and is a wonderful historic city. It is a place we hope to return to some day.

Next we went to a place in Georgia called Stone Mountain Park, located just north of Atlanta. As we neared the park entrance we were stuck in traffic on the main highway. There was an accident of several very small RVs that apparently caused a chain reaction pile up.

We finally entered the park and set up at our campsite. We sat in lawn chairs and watched as some of the injured vehicles from the accident limped into the campground. Talking with others we learned that the group was a caravan of German travelers who brought their RV's from Germany to tour the U.S. A few of the vehicles had to be towed and the rest hobbled in. What a difficult thing to endure while on vacation in a foreign land.

Stone Mountain is a large quartz monzonite dome that extends high above the treetops. On the north side of the dome is a confederate memorial carving that depicts three confederate leaders of the Civil War on horseback, Jefferson Davis, Robert E. Lee, and Stonewall Jackson. The carvings measure 90 by 190 feet and is 400 feet above the ground. A forest surrounds this rock dome. You get to the top by either sky lift or a trail. We went up the trail, after all it was only a little over a mile. How hard could that be? It was very steep and rugged, but we made it to the top and were rewarded with a cool breeze. The panoramic view was breathtaking and we could see the skyline of Atlanta in one direction and the Appalachian Mountains in the other. We sat down on top of this rocky dome and spent some time taking it all in. We returned on the same trail, which was much easier going down than it had been going up.

We also took a railroad ride around the perimeter of Stone Mountain. We ended our day watching a laser light show on the side of the dome. The light show with music, ended with fireworks. I'm glad we took this little detour in our travels, it was well worth it.

Instead of going straight to Florida, we made another big detour to Texas to spend the holidays with Don's parents. We took our time and headed west and enjoyed the time we spent with family.

Every time we start out on one of our trips we begin in Texas. After a great holiday, we traveled across Route 10 to Florida.

We were tired of moving around and wanted to pick a place that was centrally located and within a day's drive to the Gulf of Mexico and the Atlantic Ocean. Also we wanted to be far enough south to enjoy a warm winter. We chose a park located in the town of Arcadia, on the Peace River, an antique hunter's paradise. The park had a lot to offer, a pool, Laundromat, get-togethers, classes for many different interests, and entertainment.

We thought that since we were going to stay there awhile, we would get a landline phone. This would enable us to get on the internet. Don signed up for a computer class and we were set to learn a lot about this new world of computers. After only a few classes Don learned how to crash the computer! Well, I guess he did learn something. After getting our computer repaired, we bought a program called "Designing Your Own Home." Don spent a lot of time over the winter working with this program and drawing blueprints of our future house.

While we had our home base in Arcadia we managed to explore southern Florida. We took a day trip to Alligator Alley and saw 86 gators in one day. We took many day trips to the Gulf of Mexico and combed the beaches for shells. We went searching for Manatee and found them south of Arcadia in the Peace River.

We watched in amazement as some local boys fished for blue crabs. They used a clothes line rope with a piece of raw chicken tied to the end, throwing it in the water; waiting only a few minutes, then pulling up the line with the crab holding tight to the chicken. They would remove the crab and put it in their bucket and throw the same piece of chicken back into the water for another bite from a pretty blue crab.

We traveled and explored the shores of the Gulf, from Tampa to Naples. In January my brother Bob and his wife Janet and our dad came to Tampa to visit Janet's mother. We had them over for a picnic and also spent a day in Tampa visiting them. As always it was great to see family, and soon it was time again to say goodbye.

In February we spent some time on the east coast. Don signed up to work at the 24 hour Endurance Race during race week in Daytona. We packed up the RV and headed to Daytona. The workers of this event were allowed to park their RVs in a large parking lot right beside the race track. It cost $100 per night and with this price you get 24 hours of roaring car engines. What a bargain. Don would work a few hours and then come back to the camper for a break. He had a great time and as for me I slept off and on listening to the roar of the race cars. Before we returned to Arcadia we spent some time at the beach in Daytona.

In the middle of February our daughter Debbie came with a friend for a visit. She wanted to go to Key West. We locked up the Dreamcatcher and the four of us took off for a few days.

We stopped to take an airboat ride through the Everglades. They advertised that you get "up close and personal with native wildlife". We boarded the boat with many other visitors. The captain of the boat pointed out many interesting birds and wildlife of this subtropical ecosystem. He began throwing marshmallows at a large alligator named Charlie; Charlie was on the same side of the boat where Don was sitting. The captain then said for Don to be careful, that Charlie could mistake his white tee shirt for a big marshmallow. This may have been a little too "up close and personal" for us.

We made it to the southernmost point of the United States and enjoyed an evening in Key West. We booked a room at a motel within walking distance to all that Key West had to offer and then we started our tour with a bite to eat at the famous bar, "Sloppy Joes". Walking the boardwalk, we enjoyed the variety of sidewalk entertainments, and just before sunset we boarded a schooner for a sunset cruise. Beautiful evening, Beautiful boat ride, Beautiful world. Before leaving the Island of Key West we visited Fort Zachary, a civil war fort. Our last stop was at a tourist attraction where Debbie had some up close and personal time with some dolphins.

Debbie's visit was over way too soon and the rest of the winter we spent dreaming of our new home. We took several day trips and enjoyed the sunny and warm weather. It was soon spring and we began to think of heading north to Ohio.

Our last stop before Ohio was in northern Pennsylvania where my sisters and the girl members of their families meet every year near Erie, Pa, for a weekend of food, fun and lots of conversations. I had missed "Girl's Weekend" the last two years and wanted to attend this annual event. They were gathering at Peek'n Peak in southern New York. Don stayed in the Dreamcatcher in Pa. and I drove to Peek'n Peak about a half hour away. We had a great time swimming in the pool, relaxing in the hot tub, and going on walks. On Saturday evening we went to a nice restaurant and had dinner. We talked, ate and laughed.

We each wrote a little note in the guest book and signed it with our name and where we were from. I signed "the homeless sister." Having sisters and family are life's greatest blessing, and I vowed to not miss another "Girl's Weekend."

We arrived home the first week of April and again set up our camp at Clay's Park. We enjoyed the same activities as the previous summer but this time we planted a small garden behind our RV. It was great to have fresh veggies from the garden. I looked forward to planting a garden the following summer behind our new home.

We spent the summer getting things in order to start the building process. First we had to take our plans to an architect to have the blueprints made. Next was to find someone to do the construction. The same person that had built our garage agreed to build our house, although he had never built an entire house before. Did he bite off more than he could chew? Perhaps.

By Labor Day 2002, our basement was dug, and with help from our nephew Bill, and son Tim, and our builder Mike, it was soon under roof. The nights were becoming cooler and the hours of daylight shorter as the time came for us to leave the park. It was the first of November and we wanted to be near the house and assist with building our dream.

We parked the Dreamcatcher at the back of our lot and ran electric from the pole near the road.

At the time this seemed like a great solution and we would be able to watch and assist each step of the way. After all, we were in our Dreamcatcher, the place that we have called home for the last 2 1/2 years and how bad could it be in a RV, in the winter, in Ohio. We were about to find out.

As I remember it, the winter of 2002-2003 was one of the coldest and snowiest winters that we have had in a very long time. We were alone in a soybean field, with the nearest neighbor three lots away. The wind was constantly blowing and the floor of the motor home was freezing cold. We put hay bales around the bottom of the RV hoping to block the wind and maybe make it warmer, this helped very little.

About every two weeks we would drive the Dreamcatcher into town to fill up the propane tank. It was so cold that there was ice on the INSIDE of our windows. We had to carry in all our water to dump in the holding tank, and we were very conservative using it. There were a few times that we got up in the morning, turned on the faucet and nothing would come out. The pipes were frozen

189

and not a drop of water would come out of the pipes until the temperature rose slightly during the late morning. Would I live that way again? NEVER.

The inside of the house was without heat for what seemed like a long time. We used two kerosene heaters to heat the rooms while we worked. Every day was the same, wake up, eat breakfast, get dressed in our long johns and plow through the deep snow to enter a cold house and light up the heaters. By dinner time we would return to the, not so warm RV for a hot meal and an evening trying to stay warm. The work went slowly but by the beginning of March the house was almost complete. We finally had heat. The well was drilled and at last we had water. Running, HOT water. The floors had only subfloors and the walls were without paint.

We weren't allowed to move in until the final inspection was completed, but that didn't keep me from having a wonderful bubble bath in my new garden tub. The garden tub was a corner tub surrounded by beautiful tile. I lit a candle and felt as though I was washing that miserable winter down the drain.

By the first week of April, we painted the walls, laid carpet and the appliances and furniture were delivered. We moved out of what had been our RV home for the past three years. At last our dream house was complete.

Our house is a small house, just over 1600 sq. feet, but after living in an area 8 x 29 feet, it felt like a mansion. The first day I was at one end of the house and Don was at the other, when I heard him yell "Sandy, where are you?" The bigger living space would take an adjustment, but one I was ready to make. We still travel in our motor home occasionally, but now we have a place to come home to.

I hope that you have enjoyed our adventure. We feel that we have lived our dreams and made great memories that we will talk about for the rest of our days. But dreams are never done. There are always new ones waiting to be fulfilled.

Everything starts with a dream. If you don't have a dream there is no way that it can come true.

191

Dare to believe the impossible and remember "IF YOU CAN DREAM IT, YOU CAN DO IT'.

"Dream as if you will live forever, and live as if you may die tomorrow."

James Dean

Our country home

CPSIA information can be obtained
at www.ICGtesting.com
Printed in the USA
FSOW04n0713181217
42555FS

9 781481 054782